CORE
CHRISTIANITY

[What is Christianity all about?]

CORE
CHRISTIANITY

[What is Christianity all about?]

ELMER TOWNS

Advancing the Ministries of the Gospel

AMG Publishers

God's Word to you is our highest calling.

ISBN: 978-089957-109-6

First printing—March 2007

Cover designed by Daryle Beam, Bright Boy, Chattanooga, Tennessee
Interior design and typesetting by Reider Publishing Services, West Hollywood, California
Edited and Proofread by Agnes Lawless, Dan Penwell, Rich Cairnes, and Rick Steele

Printed in the United States of America
15 14   -V- 13 12

Dedicated to the Pastor's Bible Class
Thomas Road Baptist Church
Lynchburg, Virginia

I taught these lessons to the class from April 10, 2005 to July 10, 2005.

ACKNOWLEDGMENTS
I offer my sincere appreciation to
Linda Elliott and Louise Ebner for editorial assistance and
a special thank you to
Dr. Douglas Porter
for editorial assistance and consultation on
chapters three, five, six, seven, twelve, and thirteen

CONTENTS

꿍

Preface xi
From the beginning, followers of Jesus Christ have been called Christians. They are not primarily known for their doctrine or for the things they are against. These are secondary qualities. Christians are known for their relationship to Jesus Christ.

1. Christianity Is an Astonishing Person 1
The term "Christianity" is derived from the word "Christ," one of several descriptive titles describing Jesus. From the very beginning, Jesus Christ has been the heart and core of Christianity. Without Jesus, there is no Christianity.

2. Christianity Is a Life-Changing Book 15
The historic faith of Christianity grows out of a unique collection of sixty-six books, written over sixteen centuries, known popularly as the Bible. The Bible contains the revelation of God, the message of salvation, and God's purpose and plan for people on this earth. The Bible is inspired by God—without errors—and inerrant in content—accurate and reliable. Without the Bible, there is no Christianity.

3. Christianity Is an Exclusive Salvation 27
Jesus boldly told His disciples He was the exclusive way to God. The heart of the apostolic message was the

forgiveness of sins through the death of Christ. Because there was no other way to deal with humanity's sin, Christ died for us, was buried, and on the third day rose from the dead. Jesus taught that those who wanted a relationship with God could have it through Him.

4. **Christianity Is a Miraculous Resurrection**   39
Christianity is characterized by an unshakable hope in God. It grows out of one of history's greatest miracles, the resurrection of Christ from the dead. This miracle has always been a core belief of the Christian faith because it demonstrates who Christ is and what He can do for those who trust Him. Without it, there would be no Christianity.

5. **Christianity Is a Life-Transforming Experience**   51
Those who embrace Christ as their Lord and Savior are transformed through the process of conversion—involving turning from sin (repentance) to complete dependence upon Christ (saving faith). The change involved in conversion takes root in one's life and quickly becomes evident in how one lives. Those who are converted to Christ are transformed by God in their outer character and inner value system.

6. **Christianity is an Ongoing Relationship with God**   59
Christians have an ongoing experience with God that strengthens them for the various challenges they face. This experience has been described in various ways including the life of faith as a result of the unique infilling of Christ and/or the Holy Spirit. This deeper aspect of the Christian life empowers Christians for extraordinary tasks while drawing them into a closer relationship to the God they serve.

7. **Christianity Is a Disciplined Lifestyle**   69
The first term used to describe Christians in the New Testament was "disciples." At its very core, Christianity

involves the practice of spiritual disciplines that promote spiritual growth and fellowship with God. These disciplines help Christians understand the Scriptures, pray to God, develop healthy relationships with others, and impact the world in which they live with the message of the gospel and service in the community.

8. **Christianity Is a Unique Worldview**   83
   Christianity is more than an experience with God; it is also a unique way of understanding the world in which Christians live. This unique worldview is described in the New Testament as "the faith" and consists of a series of nonnegotiable values and beliefs that form a uniquely Christian view of life.

9. **Christianity Is an Interactive Community**   97
   Every Christian is exhorted to become a member of a local church, called the body of Christ. The word "church" suggests the idea of a unique community devoted to serving God and one another. The actual earthly community is reflective of a heavenly community made up of all believers. In this universal church, each believer enjoys oneness with Jesus Christ.

10. **Christianity Is a Practical Religion**   111
    Christianity makes a difference in each follower of Christ. The core values expressed by Jesus in the Sermon on the Mount will change His followers' attitudes, behavior, and character. As individuals experience God's love and understand His desire to love others through them, they experience a new desire to express their faith in practical ways.

11. **Christianity Is a Movement That Transforms Culture**   119
    Christianity influences culture in a significant way by transforming its members in a positive way. Christians advocate social justice in their culture because they

have been changed by the teachings of Christ. The abolition of slavery, prison reform, the care of widows and orphans, and the development of hospitals, orphanages, and schools are some of the historic reforms that find their source in the influence of Christianity.

12. Christianity Is a Global Directive   **133**
Christianity is not a religious heritage simply passed on from generation to generation through culture. Each person who becomes a Christian is obligated to carry out the Great Commission, which is God's plan for the evangelization of the world.

13. Christianity Is an Ultimate Hope   **147**
God has a future plan for this world and the climax of that plan is the return of Christ in power and glory to establish His kingdom. Beyond that, the Bible describes the new heaven and a new earth where believers will be resurrected to live with God forever. That enduring hope is a prime motivator in the Christian life.

Endnotes   **157**

Bibliography   **159**

PREFACE

❧

The term *Christian* occurs only three times in the Bible—Acts 11:26, Acts 26:28, and 1 Peter 4:16. The first time believers were called Christians was, in reality, a sarcastic attack: "And the disciples were first called Christians in Antioch" (Acts 11:26). The word Christian was not about doctrine, or the things Christians did. Those who were called Christians were known for their relationship to Jesus Christ.

The power of Christianity is that its followers, from the very outset, were fully persuaded that their Lord had risen from the dead and was alive; they saw Him, touched Him, and ate a meal with Him. That conviction saturated their thinking and their actions. They were so convinced that He was alive that they yearned to serve Him and even die for Him.

But the real experience of Christianity was the fact that Jesus lived in their hearts. They believed it, preached it, and everywhere they went told others about it. The indwelling presence of Christ in the lives of the Christians was the power that produced the phenomenon of the Christian church. So, Christianity is not about church buildings, creeds, or worship services. Christianity is about an astonishing Person—Jesus Christ.

The power of the indwelling Christ also motivated that first generation to proclaim the message in the immensely powerful book called the New Testament. They were inspired by the Holy Spirit to write a supernatural book, which not one of them could have written without the motivation of the resurrected Christ in them. So then, Christianity is the basis of this life-changing book.

Christianity is the throbbing life of Jesus Christ from the beginning of salvation to the end of life. Christians die victoriously looking forward to seeing Jesus in death, knowing that they'll go to live with Him for eternity.

Core Christianity is for those who know something about Christianity, but want to know more. This book is for the curious who want to know what Christianity is all about.

There are a growing number of people who have mistaken ideas about Christianity because of media bias, or because of the bad testimony of those who call themselves Christians, but don't live accordingly. Some also have a skewed view of Christianity from televangelists who seem more interested in healing, in raising money, or in outlandish emotional expressions than they are in Jesus Christ. This book builds a coherent and consistent case for the reader to understand what Christianity is. It will help Christians know what to believe so they can fulfill the admonition of Peter, "Sanctify the Lord God in your hearts, and always be ready to give a defense to everyone who asks you a reason for the hope that is in you" (1 Pet. 3:15).

Core Christianity begins with the most essential element of Christianity, which is: *Christianity Is an Astonishing Person—Jesus Christ*. Each succeeding chapter builds on the precious foundation until the last chapter—*Christianity Is an Ultimate Hope.*

My prayer is that your faith will be grounded in Scripture, your love for Christ will deepen, and you will be able to tell others what Christianity is all about.

Written from my home at the
foot of the Blue Ridge Mountains

Elmer L. Towns

1

CHRISTIANITY IS AN ASTONISHING PERSON

No other individual has impacted the history of our world in general and Western civilization in particular than Jesus of Nazareth. Although he spent much of His life in obscurity, His impact continues to this day through the religious movement that bears one of His titles. When stripped away from its various cultural expressions and practices, Christianity is ultimately the influence of a person, and that person is Jesus Christ.

Some people who don't understand Christianity think it is primarily doctrine. For them, Christianity is defined by church creeds such as the Apostles' Creed or the faith affirmation of a particular denomination with which they are acquainted. Sometimes those who define Christianity in dogmatic terms do so based on what Christians don't believe. For them, a Christian is one who does not believe in evolution, abortion, or gay marriage.

Others think of Christianity as a movement of rules defining and governing moral behavior. These rules may include prohibitions relating to drinking alcoholic beverages or using drugs, engaging in physical sexual practices before marriage, or using God's name as a curse word. They see Christianity as something designed to either take all the fun out of life or to establish boundaries to guarantee fulfillment in life.

Still others describe Christianity in terms of a specific worship experience with God. The details of that experience are as varied as those who worship as Christians. Some may describe Christianity in terms of enjoying a formal liturgical service or celebrating the Eucharist in a European cathedral. Others would deny the validity of that experience describing rather a charismatic worship service with hands raised in response to a more contemporary expression of Christian praise and worship music. Both of these groups may be real Christians, but their description of Christianity describes only outward symbols of specific expressions of Christianity. They fail to scratch below the surface to reveal the heart and soul of real Christianity.

In China today, there are an estimated hundred million believers in Jesus Christ. Because of widespread persecution throughout that nation, many of these Christians meet in homes or other designated safe places to worship. They conduct worship services without the formality of traditional liturgical worship or a worship band and praise team to lead them. And many of the indigenous hymns they sing sound different from hymns normally connected with the worship services of churches in the West. Yet their Christianity is vital, perhaps even more vital than what is found in the West. Why? Because they have Jesus Christ. He is the core of Christianity. Without Jesus Christ, there is no Christianity.

Jesus Christ ignites His followers to become obedient, so if and when godless governments demand Christians deny their faith, they willingly become martyrs. The followers of Christ sacrifice to take the message of His saving grace to uncivilized tribes, closed countries, and other villages. Because they have a personal relationship to Jesus Christ, they suffer, sacrifice, and give up everything to give the message of Jesus to others.

Today the name Jesus is among the most recognized names in the world—whether He is worshipped by Christians or used as a curse word by unbelievers. But his fame is not linked to His family background or the circumstances of His birth. Jesus was born in the obscure village of Bethlehem in southern Palestine in 4 BC to an unknown family. Yet today, one quarter of the world's people cherish the name of Jesus while, at the same time, many other religions hate His name. Jesus' birth has become the focal point of world history. All historical events are dated by His birth, either BC or AD.

Jesus was born when Roman soldiers occupied His homeland. He was born into a hated ethnic minority—the Jews. Any attention to Jesus' life and ministry should have been overshadowed by the most powerful military empire to that date, driven by their Roman laws and held together by the Roman language and civilization. The unbending Roman force ruled the world; yet, the transforming influence of this one individual—Jesus—spread internally through the hearts of Roman citizens, eventually conquering the empire when Constantine made Christianity the religion of Rome in AD 313.

Who Was Jesus?

Jesus was a real man whom the world called "the carpenter" (Mark 6:3). Many Bible teachers believe His earthly father died when Jesus was still comparatively young, so He became the family breadwinner, carrying on His father's carpentry business.

As a man, Jesus mixed freely and naturally with everyone about Him, but they didn't recognize His greatness while He was with them: "He came to His own, and His own did not receive Him" (John 1:11). Jesus ministered only about three and a half years, yet His speeches, miracles, and acts of kindness are remembered internationally today.

The Bible states Jesus was perfect in all things, yet those about Him didn't notice it, nor did they comment on it. Jesus was wonderfully balanced in personality and action. No single strength of character stands out in Him, no weakness can be seen. He had no deficiency, and didn't have to apologize for anything He said or did.

Listen to the speeches of Jesus; they were always appropriate. He never spoke when He should have been quiet, nor did He keep silent when He should have spoken.

Look at the responses of Jesus to different situations he faced in life. He always spoke the truth in love and motivated His listeners to a higher life and greater accomplishments. When His words condemned a listener, He loved those He condemned and offered them forgiveness and acceptance.

The inner strength of Jesus was never obstinate. No one could label Him "hard headed," nor was His sympathy ever "mushy emotions." He had genuine compassion for people.

While most men are known for one strength—Moses for meekness, Job for patience, and Elijah for boldness—Jesus was perfectly blended in all qualities. We cannot improve Him, redefine Him, tone down any extravagance, nor readjust any overlooked quality. Jesus was perfect!

There is no record of Jesus ever apologizing for a mistake, nor did He ever confess a sin, nor ask for forgiveness. Nothing Jesus said had to be taken back, nor did He have to redefine what He had spoken.

Jesus asked many questions of people, but He never asked for advice. He knew who He was, what He had to do on earth, and where He would go when He completed His mission on earth. It did not take long for people to see Jesus was different. The Jewish historian Josephus was a contemporary of Christ and had this to say about Him:

> Now there was about this time Jesus, a wise man, if it be lawful to call him a man, for he was a doer of wonderful works; a teacher of such men as receive the truth with pleasure. He drew over to him both many of the Jews, and many of the Gentiles. He was [the] Christ; and when Pilate, at the suggestion of the principal men amongst us, had condemned him to the cross, those that loved him at the first did not forsake him; for he appeared to them alive again the third day, as the divine prophets had foretold these and ten thousand other wonderful things concerning him; and the tribe of Christians, so named from him, are not extinct at this day.[1]

Jesus before Bethlehem

The Christmas story, the account of Jesus' physical birth in a stable in Bethlehem, is familiar to most. What many do not realize is that His birth in Bethlehem was not the beginning of His life. One of His disciples began his account of the life of Jesus with the words, "In the beginning was the

Word, and the Word was with God, and the Word was God" (John 1:1). The Bible states that Jesus was the Creator of the world with the Father and Holy Spirit (John 1:3; Col. 1:16). But if He had not existed before His birth, He could not have been the Creator.

His preexistence was not something that was blotted from His memory while on earth, for He said, "I came forth from the Father and have come into the world. Again, I leave the world and go to the Father" (John 16:28). And the night before He died, Jesus prayed for the return of the glory He had with the Father before the world existed (John 17:5).

Throughout the Old Testament, there are various accounts of God appearing to people in a physical form. Bible teachers traditionally described these appearances as *theophanies*, which literally means "appearances of God." More recently, the term *christophany* has been used because these appearances of God in the Old Testament were really preincarnate appearances of Christ.

When Jesus told the religious leaders of His day that He had seen Abraham they said, " 'You are not yet fifty years old, and have You seen Abraham?' Jesus said to them, 'Most assuredly, I say to you, before Abraham was, I AM' " (John 8:57–58). The Jewish leaders understood Jesus was calling Himself God, so they picked up stones to kill Him. But they were unable to harm Him, for He walked away through the midst of them.

The eternality of Jesus Christ is repeated by Paul, who said, "And He is before all things, and in Him all things consist" (Col. 1:17).

Once upon a Christmas

The birth of Jesus may be the most familiar aspect of the life of Jesus to many people. During the Christmas season, many people take time out of their schedule to reflect on the appearance of angels and the coming of shepherds to a stable in Bethlehem. They exchange cards with Christmas greetings and pictures of wise men and nativity scenes. When they attend seasonal Christmas services, they are again reminded of some of the historical details surrounding His birth. But often their understanding of Christmas fails to penetrate beyond the obvious to discover the more significant events that took place on that first Christmas.

There is a universal longing in the human heart to see God and make Him tangible. An early Christian leader told the Athenian philosophers of his day, "He has made us from one blood every nation of men to dwell on all the face of the earth, and has determined their preappointed times and the boundaries of their dwellings, so that they should seek the Lord, in the hope that they might grope for Him and find Him, though He is not far from each one of us" (Acts 17:26–27). This is another way of saying that everyone wants to see what God is like, and if possible, to touch God to satisfy their curiosity. Some people believe the widespread practice of worshipping idols of wood, clay, or stone is an evidence of this desire of people. Paul suggested it was the best one could do once they had rejected the truth God had already revealed to them (Rom. 1:21–23).

Because of this universal longing, "the Word [Jesus] became flesh and dwelt among us" (John 1:14). This brief statement describes what Bible teachers call the *incarnation*. This word is used to describe God becoming a man and taking on human flesh. The mystery of the incarnation implies several things about Jesus. First, it implies an existence of Christ prior to His birth. Second, it suggests some voluntary limitations of Christ as God during His life and ministry. Third, it explains why Jesus was necessarily born of a virgin rather than through the normal biological means of reproduction. Fourth, it serves as the basis for understanding the human and divine natures of Christ.

But how could the Eternal God take on human flesh? The answer to that question is found in what Bible teachers call the "kenosis." *Kenosis* is a Greek word meaning emptied. The apostle Paul used this word to describe Jesus emptying Himself to become a man (Phil. 2:7). Jesus remained God, but He emptied himself by veiling His glory, accepting the limitations of being human, and voluntarily suspending the independent use of His relative attributes. Even though John saw the glory of Jesus during his years with his Master (John 1:14), it was a veiled glory. Later, on the island of Patmos, John saw Jesus in His resurrected glory and "fell at His feet as dead" (Rev. 1:17). Although Jesus performed miracles, He was also subject to human limitations by experiencing hunger (Matt. 4:2) and thirst (John 4:6–7). Even in doing miracles, He relied on the power of the Holy Spirit to do the will of His Father (John 5:19).

Why was Jesus willing to empty Himself, setting aside all that was rightfully His to become a man? There are several reasons that may have motivated Him in this act. First, the act of sacrifice was an act of love (John 15:13). Because He loved the human race, He was prepared to become a man and go to the cross even when the world continued to reject Him (Rom. 5:8). Second, this was the best way He could reveal His Father to us (John 1:14, 18; 14:7–11). Third, it was the only way He could provide salvation to counter the effects of Adam's sin (Rom. 5:12–21). "For God so loved the world that He gave His only begotten Son, that whoever believes in Him should not perish but have everlasting life" (John 3:16). He also humbled Himself as an example for us to follow (Phil. 2:5).

When an individual understands the deity of Jesus—that He is God—it becomes easier to understand why He was miraculously conceived in a virgin. The fact that Jesus was born of a virgin doesn't mean that He was born in a different manner than anyone else. Indeed, He had a normal delivery as every other baby in the world. The miracle was His conception by the Holy Spirit in the womb of the Virgin Mary. That means that she had not sexually known any man. When the human race fell into sin, God offered hope in "the seed of the woman" (Gen. 3:15). Later, Isaiah prophesied, "Behold, the virgin shall conceive and bear a Son, and shall call His name Immanuel" (Isa. 7:14). In the New Testament, Matthew, Luke, and Paul each describe the virgin birth of Jesus (Matt. 1:25; Luke 1:27; 3:23; Gal. 4:4).

The result of the virgin birth is that Jesus was born with the human nature of His mother and the divine nature of His Father. He did not inherit the sin nature that the human race inherits from ones' fathers because His Father was God. The Scriptures are very clear concerning the absence of sin in the life of Jesus. Christ knew no sin (2 Cor. 5:2), was without sin (Heb. 4:15), committed no sin (1 Pet. 2:22), and there was no sin found in Him (1 John 3:5).

When Christian leaders tried to explain the relationship between the human and divine natures of Jesus at the

Council of Chalcedon in AD 451, they issued a statement that described Jesus as "made known in two natures without confusion, without change, without division, without separation, the distinction of natures being by no means taken away by the union." When Jesus became a man, He remained God while also becoming human. Neither of these natures was in any way corrupted or altered in the process.

Some critics of Christianity erroneously claim the Council of Chalcedon is where the church made Jesus into God. That conclusion is inconsistent with both the context and conclusions of the council. The council sought to clarify an issue of faith historically held by Christians from the first century because some teachers were advocating a view different from that historically believed. If their goal was to simply make Jesus into God, it would have better suited their purpose to issue a statement declaring His deity and denying His humanity. They did not issue such a statement because that was not their agenda.

The Bible has several things to say about this unique union of two natures. Jesus was completely human and completely divine. This union of natures was complete, not partial, and was permanent (Heb. 13:8). Finally, this union of natures has continued beyond the resurrection of Christ. Today, "the man Christ Jesus" acts as our mediator before God the Father (1 Tim. 2:5).

The incarnation of Christ gives special meaning and significance to Christmas. The Christmas season celebrates the moment in human history when "the Word became flesh" to confirm God's promises (Rom. 15:8; Matt. 5:17), reveal the Father (John 1:18), become a faithful high priest

(Heb. 5:1; 7:25), put away sin (Gen. 22:8; John 1:29), destroy the works of Satan (1 John 3:8), and provide an example for believers to follow (1 John 2:6; 1 Pet. 2:21).

How Did Jesus Live?

If ever there was a perfect baby, Jesus was that child. And He developed in four areas. "And Jesus increased in wisdom and stature, and in favor with God and men" (Luke 2:52). First, Jesus grew in wisdom; that meant He had to learn words, put thoughts together and grow in understanding. Next, He increased in stature. He had to eat to remain healthy, to grow His muscles, and develop His physical stamina. In the third area, Jesus increased in favor with God, which is spiritual development. Finally, Jesus grew socially, increasing in favor with man.

At age thirty (Luke 3:23), Jesus was baptized by John the Baptist, even though the Baptist did not want to do it. Jesus told him, "It must be done, because we must do everything that is right" (Matt 3:15). As a result, Jesus identified with those who chose to follow Him.

And at the beginning of Jesus' ministry Satan tempted Him on three occasions to sin: "He was in all points tempted as we are, yet without sin" (Heb. 4:15). Because Jesus had fasted for forty days and was hungry, He was vulnerable to temptation. Yet Jesus refused to make stones into bread, He refused to worship Satan, who promised to give Him the kingdoms of the earth, and Jesus didn't give into the pride of life by casting Himself off the temple pinnacle so angels could rescue Him. Jesus was tempted in all points of His humanity, but He didn't sin.

Jesus Was God

Jesus began His ministry in obscurity walking across the dusty roads of the Holy Land, but eventually became one of the best-known persons of all times; and He continues to walk across the pages of history. And if Jesus were not God, Christianity would not have become the powerful force in the world it is. Lord Byron the English poet said, "If ever a man was God, or God was man, Jesus was both."[2]

On many occasions Jesus said He was God. If He were not, then He is a blasphemer. But still, the critics say Jesus is only a good man because He did many kind deeds for people. If He were not God, then He is a blasphemer for claiming to be God, which means He cannot be good. If He were not God, then He is a shameless impostor. Didn't Jesus claim, "He who has seen Me has seen the Father" (John 14:9)? And didn't Jesus openly boast, "I and the Father are one?" (John 10:30).

But perhaps the greatest boast of all is when Jesus constantly claimed to be the great "I AM." The word LORD, or Jehovah, is the primary name for deity in the Old Testament. It comes from the verb to be, "I AM," repeated twice. Who can deny Jesus said constantly, "I am the bread of life" (John 6:35), "I am the light of the world" (John 8:12), "I am the door" (John 10:9), "I am the good shepherd" (John 10:11), "I am the resurrection and the life" (John 11:25), and "I am the way, the truth and the life" (John 14:6)? The infuriated Jews constantly tried to kill Him, because they rejected what they thought were Jesus' blasphemous statements.

His many names point to Jesus' deity. He wasn't called Jonah, Abel, or Henry. He fulfilled the Old Testament prediction, "They shall call His name Immanuel, which is translated, 'God with us' " (Matt. 1:23, predicted in Isaiah 7:14). The angel told Mary to call His name Jesus, which means, "Jehovah saves." Look at His other names and titles: Redeemer, Savior, Son of God, King, Cornerstone, Alpha and Omega, and the Almighty. One source lists over eight hundred names, titles, metaphors, and symbols to represent Jesus.[3] Why so many? Because these names are descriptive of His character and the work He does for all humanity.

The miracles of Jesus point to His deity. Who does the works of God, but God Himself? Listen to the man born blind testify, "I was blind but now I see" (John 9:25). Take note of the voice of the cleansed leper crying out, "Jesus, Master, have mercy on us . . . when he saw that he was healed, returned, and with a loud voice glorified God, and fell down on his face at His feet, giving Him thanks" (Luke 17:13–16). Look at Lazarus dead four days, but he comes out of the tomb resurrected and ready to live again (John 11:1–44). Ask 5,000 people if they enjoyed their dinner miraculously provided from five loaves and two fishes (John 6:1–14).

And finally, Jesus did something that no right-thinking human would ever do: Jesus received worship. "And behold, a leper came and worshiped Him" (Matt 8:2). And the demoniac of Gadera came and worshiped Jesus after the demons were cast out (Mark 5:6). After Jesus had walked upon the water and calmed the storms, the disciples worshiped Him (Matt. 14:33). Who else would receive worship but God?

Think about It

Question: If God became human, wouldn't He tell everyone He was God?

Answer: Jesus called Himself, "The light of the world," so we naturally expect Him to shine and illuminate everything around Him. Therefore, Jesus told everyone who He was, and why He came into the world. Jesus is Creator of the world, the Second Person of the Trinity, and the Savior of the world. He is the Lord Jesus Christ, the core of Christianity. There is no Christianity without Him.

2

❧

CHRISTIANITY IS A LIFE-CHANGING BOOK

All that Christianity is can be found in the Bible. If there were no Bible, there wouldn't be a life-transforming religion called Christianity.

Christianity is more than doctrinal belief, and the Bible is more than a theology textbook. Christianity is more than Ten Commandments and regulations, and the Bible is more than a rule book. The transforming life of Christianity springs from the pages of a life-producing book—the Bible.

I have a friend, Bob, who went through high school in the 1940s in a large California city. Bob told me how his father hated everything about Christianity. He tore pages out of any magazine that featured Christianity, and abruptly changed the radio station if he heard anything religious.

In college, Bob took a sophomore literature course in history's great books. He was infuriated because he had to read and report on the Gospel of John (in the Bible). Confronting his teacher, Bob declared he would not read anything from the Bible because it was filled with myths, mistakes, and man's opinion.

"You're prejudiced," the teacher answered, then pointed out other books he had to read that told of Greek myths, and the lies of Adolph Hitler's *Mein Kampf*. The teacher instructed him, "Read to find out why these books have changed the course of history—not because they are right or wrong, and not because you agree with them."

"Oh," is all Bob could say.

Bob faced his prejudice and determined to read the Gospel of John to see what Jesus said and why the Bible changed the flow of history. He found his roommate's New Testament, received from the Gideons. To maintain his atheistic reputation, he locked the door so no one would see him with any part of the Bible. So, Bob began to read and take notes. He filled his empty mind with the transforming words of Jesus, which he had never heard. He filled his notebook with compelling reasons why Jesus changed the course of history.

Bob's academic mind was engaged as he read it all the way through in one sitting. Then he began reading it again; this time he engaged his heart. Bob liked this fellow Jesus, but couldn't understand why he didn't escape the cross. Still in one sitting, Bob began reading it the third time, but this time he was a hungry seeker. He was having a spiritual experience with God.

Finally, Bob knelt by his bed, and looked to heaven (he hadn't been instructed to close his eyes). He didn't know how to repent, address God, or pray the sinner's prayer. Bob confessed he was saved when he prayed,

"I believe!"

Bob went on to graduate from a theological seminary and became a minister for God. What the Bible did for Bob Hamilton, it has done for millions who have had their life transformed by its message. Why is that? Because the Bible is a book that records God's revelation of Himself to His people. It is not a mystery with intelligible words or far-fetched mantras, or inconceivable events such as people turning to animals, or flying horses. The Bible tells the story of real people doing real things in normal ways. It tells of good people and their desire to know God and serve Him. It doesn't omit the bad things that some of these good people do. The Bible describes their faith in God and tells how people today can exercise that same kind of faith to experience the presence of God in their lives.

The Bible relates how God intercepted the lives of people to save them from disaster and to show them a better way to live. And those who read the Bible can experience the same guidance in their lives. The Bible explains how God sent His servants to give a message to His people. This was a message of salvation from sin, a warning against trespassing against His laws, directions on how an individual should live, and the way a person should worship Him. Those who read the Bible today get the same benefits.

But the Bible is more than the story of God; when you read it you are listening to God, for the Bible is God's Word. Just as some in the past heard the audible voice of God, so you hear Him speak to your heart through the Bible.

The Bible is distinct from other religious books. Books of other religions were written by their founders in their attempt to find God. They were searching for God and their books tell of their thoughts and conclusions. Their writings want people to follow their example to find God, and they describe how the readers are to act or react. But the Bible is not a search for God; the Bible is God's book to reveal Himself to the human race.

The Bible is composed of sixty-six books or letters all bound into one volume. It was written over a period of 1,600 years by approximately forty writers of various occupations, spread out over 2,200 miles between two continents, and from more than a dozen countries; yet the Bible is held together by a single theme. And no matter where a person reads, he will find the authority of God. Often the Bible says, "Thus saith the Lord" or "The Word of the Lord came to me." Thus, the Bible is God speaking personally to each individual.

But even though there are approximately forty writers from various backgrounds, the Bible has an undeniable single purpose: "Men were under the control of the Holy Spirit as they spoke the message that came from God" (2 Peter 1:21, TEV).

So when you read the Bible you're left with the impression that only one person wrote the Bible. How is that possible?

The Bible was written by *dual authors*. This means that both God and man were writing the Bible at the same time. When the Bible says, "All scripture is given by inspiration of God" (2 Tim. 3:16), the word inspiration comes from *theo*, which is God, and *pneuma*, which is to breathe. Therefore, when an author was writing the Bible, God breathed into the author's life the words and messages to be written down. Each author chose words and wrote sentences that expressed his thoughts, but every word and every thought written on the page was God's Word.

When the physician, Luke, wrote the book of Acts, he interviewed Paul and others to write the stories of planting new churches, but at other times, Luke was an eyewitness and wrote what he saw. But no matter the source of what Luke wrote, the Holy Spirit was breathing into him the words and messages so that what he wrote was what God wanted him to write (Luke 1:1–4).

Since God cannot tell a lie or mislead people, the Bible will not lie to a person or lead that individual astray. The Bible accurately does include the lies told by individuals, but readers need to know that they are not to believe the lie when they read it. The Bible is accurate because God is truth and does all things accurately. The Bible declares of itself, "The writings of the Lord are true and righteous altogether" (Ps. 19:9, author translation).

The Bible is supernatural in focus. No matter where an individual reads, it points to Jesus Christ. The entire Old Testament points to the coming of Jesus Christ, who fulfilled the promises God made to His servants. "Long ago God spoke many times and in many ways to our ancestors through the prophets. And now in these final days, he has spoken to us through his Son. God promised everything to the Son as an inheritance, and through the Son he created the universe" (Heb. 1:1–2, NLT).

A. M. Hodgkin in his book, *Christ in All the Scriptures,* shows how every verse in the Bible points to Jesus Christ.[4] Sometimes Christ is seen by direct reference, other times by prediction, type, symbol, or metaphor; but Christ is seen throughout the Scriptures. How can that happen? Because the Bible is supernaturally written by God to tell the human race what He is like.

Technically, the word *Bible* is not found in the actual text of the Bible; it's only found on the cover and title page of the Bible. When the Old Testament first appeared, men of God wrote the message down on leather, also called vellum or parchments. These were the fine soft skins of animals sewn together, one after another, and rolled into a scroll.

In the synagogue of Jesus' day, there were probably three scrolls in a large wooden box or pot near the podium. The first scroll was noted as the words of *Moses* and was made up of the five books written by Moses. The second was noted as the words of the *Prophets* and contained the Major Prophets. The third was noted as the words of the *Psalms* because *Psalms* occurred first, but this scroll also included the historical books and Minor Prophets. Notice Jesus referred to these divisions of the Old Testament when He said to the disciples in the Upper Room, "These are the words which I spoke to you while I was still with you, that all things must be fulfilled which were written in the Law of Moses and the Prophets and the Psalms concerning Me" (Luke 24:44).

A few of the New Testament books were written on parchment and rolled into scrolls. However, the church soon began using paper made from papyrus reeds grown in swampy areas. The soft milky core was flattened out by pounding on a stone, then dried into sheets. Since these sheets cracked when rolled, they were kept flat and sewn together at the edges, thus making a book with a spine. This was the first appearance of what we call a book. Technically, these were called *codex*, the first title for these books.

On the outside cover was written *ta biblia*, which simply means "the book." To the early church, all sixty-six books were simply "The Book," the book of God, or the book of salvation. The Latin, *ta biblia*, became *Bible* in English. Later, the word *holy* was added to *Bible* and thus one finds on the front cover, the *Holy Bible*. Since the word *holy* means separated to God. For that reason the *Holy Bible* is a book from God and dedicated to God's use.

A few people called the Bible the *Scriptures*. This is from the word *scriptus,* which is the act of producing writing. Consequently, the Bible is the writings of God.

Other people call the Bible the *Word of God,* which means this book has the words from God, and the words about God. When Jesus returns at the end of time, the phrase "the Word of God" is embroidered on His garments, showing the importance God places on the words of Scripture (Rev. 19:13, KJV).

The Bible Breathes Life into People

The Bible is much more than an accurate textbook that tells about God's people in the Old and New Testaments. Because it is accurate, we can rely on its message; but there's another supernatural aspect of the Bible. When God breathed into the authors the Word of God, the words they wrote had the "breath of God" in them.

Because God is eternal, you get eternity into your heart when you read and believe the Bible's words. This is why Peter said to Jesus, "Thou hast the words of eternal life" (John 6:68). Because God is life, when you read and believe its words you get the very life of God in your soul. Jesus said, "The words that I speak to you are spirit, and [they] are life" (John 6:63).

Remember, Jesus is called the Word of God: "In the beginning was the Word, and the Word was with God, and the Word was God" (John 1:1). Both Jesus and the Bible are called the Word, but there is a difference. Jesus is the *incarnate* Word from God who clothed Himself with flesh and blood so the human race could see what God was like. The Bible is the *inspired* Word from God written on pages to tell humanity what God is like. Yes, both are *the Word*. The Word convicts of sins, exposes error, invites people to God, tells of salvation, gives eternal life, and assures the believer of his relationship to God.

Because the Bible is supernatural, it can transform the reader. Peter noted that a person is converted through the Bible, "being born again . . . by the Word" (1 Peter 1:23). Therefore, do more than read the Bible to learn accurate facts about what Jesus did on earth, and do more than study the Bible to learn the content of Christian doctrine. As you read the Word, make it a part of your life. Christ enters your life through the Word so you can be born again and receive the life of God.

The Bible Is the Most Influential Book in History

The Bible has been translated into every language in the civilized world, though there are still approximately 9,000 uncivilized tribal languages into which the Bible has not yet been translated. When the Bible was translated into the languages of uncivilized tribes, individuals were converted to Christianity and slowly the tribes became civilized. Missionaries from organizations such as Wycliffe Bible Translators have gone to heathen tribes, learned their language, and reduced it into letters, words, and sentences. Then they translated the Bible into the language of the people and taught them to read the Bible.[5] When member after member of a heathen tribe has heard the Bible and made it a part of their life, they want a better life. This is technically called *redemption and lift*. God redeems His people, and they lift themselves to a higher level of civilization.

Eventually the Bible civilizes a tribe so they live on a higher level than before. Wherever the Bible goes, culture and civilization shortly follow.

The Bible has influenced some of the greatest leaders in the world. John Adams wrote an entry in his diary February 22, 1756,

> Suppose a nation in some distant region should take the Bible for their only law book, and every member should regulate his conduct by the precepts there contained! Every member would be obliged in conscience to temperance, frugality and industry: to justice, kindness and charity towards his fellow men: and to piety, love and reverence toward Almighty God . . . . What a Eutopia, what a Paradise would this region be.[6]

The Bible has been one of the greatest motivators of those who believe its contents. Christian leaders have lived by the Bible, taught the Bible, and given their lives to master the Bible. No other religion has produced as many books to explain itself, or beautiful paintings and works of art to express its message, or pieces of sculpture to reflect its people, or music to reflect its emotions and message

The Greatness of the Bible

The Bible is a great book because it tells the truth about the sinfulness of the human race. It teaches that no matter how good an individual is outwardly, he is a sinner and short of God's standards. At the end of his life, Paul could testify, "Christ Jesus came into the world to save sinners, of whom I am chief" (1 Tim. 1:15).

The Bible never flinches to when telling the bad news about good men. It tells how Abraham, the man of faith couldn't trust God so he lied. It relates how David, a man after God's own heart, committed adultery with Bathsheba. It tells how Peter, the bold fisherman, denied Jesus three times. The list could go on because the Bible tells the truth about the faults of God's leaders. Yet, the normal reader doesn't read about the sin of Noah getting drunk, then go out to do the same. Nor does one read about Solomon's many wives and follow his example. No, the Bible is a truthful book that looks beyond the sins of its people to the truth it upholds.

Perhaps the greatest influence of the Bible is its convicting, convincing, converting power to all who honestly accept its message and believe in Jesus Christ. When I was an ordinary high school student, I cussed as much as the average guy. I told lies to keep out of trouble: "Yes, ma'am, I did my homework but I left it at home." In my heart I knew I lied, because normal people can't lie to themselves. I had immoral thoughts and a vicious temper. Yet, the Bible *convicted* me of my sin, *convinced* me to seek Jesus Christ as Savior, and *converted* me when I asked Jesus to come into my heart.

And what were the results of my conversion? God transformed my mouth; I didn't curse any longer. I began memorizing Scripture that changed my desires about sin, and I had an overwhelming desire to serve God.

Finally, the Bible is a story of present hope for those who are discouraged, despondent, or have no purpose in life. The Bible states that God loves the whole human race and has a wonderful plan for each individual life. The Bible is a story of the future when Christ will return to take His people to be with Him. When an individual has died, his body will be resurrected, and he will live with God for all eternity.

Individuals can't have Christianity without a person— Jesus Christ. And they can't have Christianity without a book—the Bible.

Think about It

Question: How can anyone know the Bible is God's Word?

Answer: It is impossible to convince the mind through reason alone that the Bible is God's book. Salvation involves all aspects of a person's personality. You must know (with your mind) the facts of your lost condition and that Jesus died for you. Second, you must feel (with your emotions) sorrow for sinning against God, as well as love for Him because of what Christ has done for you. Third, you must choose (with your will) to put your trust in Christ to save you from your sin.

Accepting the Bible as the Word of God follows the same three steps of choice. You must honestly examine the facts regarding the Bible. Next you must face your emotions. Has the Bible stirred your feelings for God? Finally, you must choose whether you will or will not believe.

The best way to demonstrate that the Bible is the Word of God is to put God's promises to the test. Just as you know a pie is good by eating, so you will know God is real by experiencing the benefits of His Word. Just as you must follow a road to find out if it will lead to a destination, so apply the directions of the Bible to your life. Jesus said, "The one who comes to Me I will by no means cast out" (John 6:37). When you apply the Bible to your life, you will experience the benefits it promises.

3

CHRISTIANITY IS AN EXCLUSIVE SALVATION

What is so amazing about the fact that Jesus died? Buddha died in 480 BC, Confucius died in 479 BC, and Muhammad died in AD 632. As one knows, death is inevitable to everyone in the human race. The Scriptures teach, "It is appointed for men to die once" (Heb. 9:27).

But the death of Jesus Christ was far different from the death of any other religious leader. Jesus died for the sins of the world; now all people can call on the Lord to forgive their rebellion against Him. "For God so loved the world that He gave His only begotten Son, that whoever believes in Him should not perish but have everlasting life" (John 3:16). The death of Jesus provides more than just the forgiveness of sin. When people become Christians, their whole life is transformed.

I was a typical high school boy growing up in Savannah, Georgia, with a paper route to make spending money. I went to Sunday school and knew about God. I even joined the church and everyone thought I was going to heaven. But in my heart I knew I was lost.

In the spring of 1944, I was one attending one of about twelve youth attending a catechism class preparing for church membership. The preacher went around the class asking each one if they believed in a certain doctrine. Then he asked the rest of us if we agreed. Each time I nodded my head "yes." Yes, I believed the facts of Christianity.

The preacher asked if we believed in the virgin birth of Christ. I was not sure what a virgin was, but I knew it was taught in the Bible so I nodded "yes."

The last question was about the second coming of Jesus Christ. When the preacher asked the class if we believed that Jesus was coming again, I once more nodded "yes." But in my heart, I knew I wasn't ready to meet the Lord. Many times while riding my bike to deliver newspapers I'd cry out, "Lord, save me." But each time I didn't feel saved.

In July of 1950, I attended a revival meeting at the Bonna Bella Presbyterian Church, a mission of my home church. God was working in the hearts of many in that community, and I could feel it. Each night five to twelve people were being saved, and the revival stretched into a second week.

On Thursday evening, July 25, no one came forward to give their life to the Lord. The pastor came to the front of the auditorium, looked everyone in the eye, and said, "Someone here is refusing to come forward and you're breaking the momentum of the revival." I knew the minister was talking to me. He gave these simple instructions, "Go home and kneel by your bed, look to God in heaven, and make this prayer: 'Lord Jesus, I've never done it before; I am lost. Come into my heart and save me.'"

I went home and knelt by my bed, but was reluctant to pray because I had joined the church. I thought I was good enough. So, I prayed the Lord's Prayer and got in bed. But conviction wouldn't let me go to sleep. I got out of bed to kneel a second time, but I still couldn't pray what I was told. So I prayed, "Now I lay me down to sleep, I pray the Lord my soul to keep . . ."

I got back in bed, but tossed and turned under severe conviction of sin. So I got out of bed, looked out my window into heaven and prayed, "Lord Jesus, I've never done this before; I am lost . . ." When I said those words, I felt the horrors of hell. I felt as though I were already in hell. I suffered for a few agonizing seconds and then quickly cried out, "Lord Jesus, come into my heart and save me." He did, and I knew it. I knew I was saved as much as a blind man knows when he receives sight. The blind man said, "Once I was blind, but now I can see." But I could say, "Once I was lost, but now I am saved."

An Exclusive Salvation

Those who believe in Jesus Christ make the exclusive claim that His death provided the only way of salvation, they point to His declaration, "I am the way, the truth, and the life. No one comes to the Father except through Me" (John 14:6). Jesus died as "the Lamb of God who takes away the sin of the world!" (John 1:29). As a matter of fact, there would be no Christianity if Jesus had not died in this particular way and for this specific purpose.

The untimely end of Jesus on the cross was not a pitiful death. By the word *pitiful* we express sympathy to one suffering an unjust consequence. The death of Jesus was victorious. The Bible asks, "O Death, where is your sting? O Hades, where is your victory?" (1 Cor. 15:55). What did the death of Christ give us? "Thanks be to God, who gives us the victory through our Lord Jesus Christ" (1 Cor. 15:57).

Being crucified at age thirty-three, some think Jesus died too soon, before He could live out the normal adult life. But Jesus' death was not an unfortunate event. His death was predicted in the Old Testament and the events surrounding His death were also predicted: "When the fullness of the time had come, God sent forth His Son . . . to redeem those who were under the law" (Gal. 4:4–5).

The death of Jesus was not a disappointing death. Oh yes, women wept as they viewed the Crucifixion from afar. Isn't death always a painful separation? Everyone who loved Jesus was apparently disappointed. They didn't realize at the time that His death would give life to the world.

The death of Jesus on the cross was predicted in the Old Testament, even though crucifixion was not used for capital punishment by Rome for another 1,400 years. The Bible foretold of one who would "hang on a tree." Then it explained, "He that is hanged is accursed of God" (Deut. 21:22–23, author translation). The New Testament confirms this was a reference to Jesus' death: "Christ . . . being made a curse for us" (Gal. 3:13, author translation).

Jesus being made a curse for all humankind is the secret of Christ's death, and why His crucifixion has touched the world. He died as a substitute in the place of every person. This substitutionary death had been predicted in Isaiah 53: "He was wounded for our transgressions" (Isa. 53:5).

The cross did not slip up on Jesus unexpectedly. He knew what terrible suffering lay ahead because He prayed, "Let this cup pass from Me" (Matt. 26:39). Jesus knew He faced excruciating torture and prolonged physical suffering. He knew that Roman soldiers would beat him terribly,

"Pilate . . . scourged Him" (John 19:1). Scourging was either by rods that left deep welts on the body or by a cat-o'-nine-tails that ripped the flesh to pieces. Jesus endured both.

Since Jesus was God and knew all things that would happen to Him (John 13:1), why didn't He prevent His crucifixion? Why didn't He use His power to stop His sufferings? Jesus told Pilate, His judge, "Do you think that I cannot now pray to My Father, and He will provide Me with more than twelve legions of angels? (Matt. 26:53). Jesus didn't prevent His death because of His love for those for whom He died. First, He loved His disciples, "Having loved His own . . . He loved them to the end" (John 13:1). All of this, "because He first loved us" (1 John 4:19).

There is the secret of Christ's death, because Christ died as a substitute in the place of every individual.

Technically, the death of Jesus was capital punishment for alleged crimes against Rome. Just as America generally uses lethal injection and the French Revolution used the guillotine, so Romans used the cross as the ultimate punishment for crimes against the state. They made the suffering ghastly to scare the masses into obeying their laws.

However, the trial of Jesus Christ was a study of contradictions. Witnesses disagreed, the charge against Him was changed in the middle of the trial, and the judge found Him innocent. And yet, they still executed Jesus. In America today, even the scarcest breach of legal justice will free a person from languishing on death row, but no such exemption was made for Jesus Christ. Even the trial judge, Pilate, after listening to all the evidence said, "I find no fault in Him" (John 19:6). And did Pilate let Him go? No! Pilate gave in to the pressure of the accusers and allowed Jesus to be executed: "You take Him and crucify [Him]" (John 19:6). What seemed like total barbarity by men was part of the divine plan of God. "When they had come to the place called Calvary, there they crucified Him" (Luke 23:33).

Events Surrounding the Death of Jesus Christ

Jesus was crucified on a small hill outside Jerusalem, a place called "*the Place* of a skull, which is called in Hebrew, Golgotha" (John 19:17). He was executed in public. This was Rome's way of intimidating the rest of the population to obey their laws.

Jesus was crucified early on Friday before the Jewish Passover: "It was nine o'clock in the morning when the crucifixion took place" (Mark 15:25, NLT).

Just as Jesus had been the center of attraction when He taught and healed, He also became the center of attention in His crucifixion: "There they crucified Him, and the criminals, one on the right hand and the other on the left" (Luke 23:33).

The Jews accused Jesus of blasphemy, "because He made Himself the Son of God" (John 19:7). Pilate wouldn't accept this charge because it was a religious argument, not a violation of Roman law. Then contrary to law, in the middle of the trial, the Jews changed their accusation to treason: "Whosoever makes himself a king speaks against Caesar" (John 19:12).

When a man was crucified, the charge against him was usually written on a small piece of board, similar to a wood shingle, and nailed above his head on the cross. Pilate directed the sign to read—JESUS OF NAZARETH, KING OF THE JEWS (John 19:19). When the Jews saw it, they were horrified at the bold announcement. They tried to get Pilate to change it so it would read, "He said I am King of the Jews." But Pilate refused with his famous reply, "What I have written, I have written" (John 19:22). Providentially, God announced to the world that His Son was the King of the Jews and in so doing, God pointed out the irony that Jews were crucifying their King.

While Jesus was on the cross, nature erupted. "It was noon, and darkness fell across the whole land" (Luke 23:44). It's as though God in heaven refused to look upon the travesty that was unfolding on Golgotha. God turned away from Jesus Christ, so that Jesus cried out, "My God, My God, why have You forsaken Me?" (Matt. 27:46). Just as the wind stiffens in the cool of the evening, the tunics of those crucifying Jesus flapped in the breeze as the death wind whipped across Calvary.

And there were other phenomena. "At that moment the curtain in the Temple was torn in two, from top to bottom. The earth shook, rocks split apart" (Matt. 27:51, NLT). The curtain was a symbolic barrier between God and man, keeping people from looking to the presence of God in the Holy of Holies. The death of Jesus removed the barrier between God and man: "He . . . has broken down the middle wall of separation" (Eph. 2:14).

The death of Jesus had a profound impact on those who were watching. One thief being crucified turned against Jesus, cursing both Jesus and God. He died in his sins. The other thief repented, crying out, "Lord, remember me when You come into Your kingdom" (Luke 23:42). We know his repentance was real, for Jesus said to him, "Assuredly, I say to you, today you will be with Me in

Paradise" (Luke 23:43). This statement reflects that Jesus knew He would die and be in Paradise later that day, so He assured the thief that He, too, would join him there.

The centurion who was supervising the soldiers crucifying Jesus also realized this death was a travesty of injustice. After witnessing all that transpired, he fell to his knees crying, "Truly this was the Son of God!" (Matt. 27:54).

Two men who were secret believers went to ask Pilate for the body. The first was Joseph of Arimathea, a rich ruler in the city of Jerusalem, and with him came Nicodemus, a religious ruler of the Jews. Pilate was surprised at the request and sent a soldier to verify the fact that He had died. Soldiers would usually take the large mallet with which they drove the spikes and shatter the knees and legs of the victims to hasten death. This assured the victim's death so the soldiers could leave and return to their barracks. But notice when they came to Jesus, they saw that He was dead already, so they didn't break His legs. This is important because it fulfills Old Testament prediction. "For these things were done that the Scripture should be fulfilled, 'Not one of His bones shall be broken' " (John 19:36, Ex. 12:46, Num. 9:12, Ps. 34:20).

However, the soldiers wanted to make sure that He was dead so one of them took his spear and thrust it into the side of Jesus, piercing the heart sac. But something happened inside the body of Jesus. "Immediately blood and water came out" (John 19:34). Medical authorities have said that at the point of death, blood and water in the heart sac separate so that when the body is pierced, the two liquids come out separately.

Joseph and Nicodemus took the body of Jesus and buried Him. "Then they took the body of Jesus, and bound it in strips of linen with the spices" (John 19:40). Joseph of Arimathea like most rich men had carved a sepulcher in preparation for his burial, but instead of using it for himself, he put Jesus in his tomb in a garden near Golgotha: "So there they laid Jesus" (John 19:42).

- A new tomb carved recently (John 19:40)
- A borrowed tomb, from Joseph (Matt. 27:60)
- Never used and undefiled (Luke 23:53)

A group of women had followed Jesus because they loved Him and believed in His message. However, these women didn't come to the brow of Golgotha, perhaps because of natural fear of the soldiers. They were eyewitnesses, having observed the tomb and how His body was laid (Luke 23:55). Two of these women were identified, "And Mary Magdalene and Mary the mother of Joses observed where He was laid" (Mark 15:47).

Because the Jews began their Sabbath at sundown on Friday, the women being sensitive to the Law did not come to anoint the body of Jesus that evening or during the Sabbath. They waited until early Sunday morning to return to the tomb (Mark 16:1). One can only imagine what went through their minds on that torturous weekend as they contemplated that their Savior was dead and buried in a cold tomb. But like so many with limited perspective, they didn't realize the complete purpose of the death, nor did they understand the transforming prospects of the resurrection they would witness on Sunday morning.

The deceitful Jewish leaders, who had gone to excessive lengths to make sure Jesus was crucified, now went to extreme lengths to make sure that the body would stay in the grave. They were afraid that the disciples might come and steal the body, then tell everybody that He had been raised from the dead (Matt. 27:62, 64). So, the Jewish leaders asked Pilate for governmental security for Jesus' grave. First, they placed an official seal on the stone that covered the grave (Matt. 27:65). The seal was not like a padlock to keep people out but was more like yellow tape at crime scenes used by police today to warn trespassers against entrance. Those who broke the seal would be indicted and punished under Roman law. But the seal was not enough.

Then, they "set the guard" (Matt. 27:66) so that soldiers guarded the tomb to keep everyone away. Even though unbelieving men had done everything they could to secure the body of Jesus, what they didn't count on was the power of God, "For an angel of the Lord descended from heaven, and came and rolled back the stone from the door, and sat on it" (Matt. 28:2).

This chapter deals only with the benefits for the death of Christ, but in the next chapter, I will examine the supernatural benefits of His resurrection.

Some think Jesus' death was comparable to Davy Crockett's, who died fighting in the Alamo, because his cause was just and his death inspired the Texans to a future victory over the invading Mexican army of Santa Anna. But the death of Jesus was not just a martyr's death whereby Jesus laid down His life for the cause for which He had preached. No! Jesus' death was much more than an example to inspire His followers.

Jesus died a substitutionary death. In other words, He took the place of those who should have died. Because "all have sinned and fall short of the glory of God" (Romans 3:23), then all should be punished by God for breaking His law. But Jesus took the punishment of all. Notice the all-inclusive nature of His death: "Behold! The Lamb of God who takes away the sin of the world!" (John 1:29).

But obviously, not everyone in the world is saved, and not everyone will go to heaven because of the death of Jesus. It has been said that the death of Jesus is *sufficient* for all, but it is *efficient* only for those who believe in Him. Therefore, Jesus is the actual substitute for those who believe in Him. "Christ also loved the church and gave Himself for her" (Eph. 5:25). To make sure that people understand the application of the death of Christ in their life, notice what Paul said: "The Son of God . . . gave Himself for me" (Gal. 2:20).

Next, the death of Jesus was a redemptive death. The word *redeemed* means "bought back." In America, we have pawn shops where people needing money sell something to a pawn broker. Then, when they get money, they go to "buy back" their possession from the pawn broker. This is called redeeming a possession. When Jesus died, He redeemed His people. Originally, everyone belonged to Him. Didn't God create all men in His image, and didn't all people belong to Him before they sinned? When the human race rebelled against God, they were put under the judgment of the Law. And what did the death of Christ accomplish? "Christ hath redeemed us from the curse of the law" (Gal. 3:13).

Redemption took place because the death of Christ satisfied the Law against us. God had to punish everyone who sins against Him, but Christ died to satisfy the punishment. It's similar to a speeding ticket. When a person is caught breaking the law by speeding, he must pay a fine to satisfy the charge against him. The good news is that Jesus paid your fine. The Bible calls this *propitiation*, which means to satisfy. (He) "sent His Son to be the propitiation for our sins" (1 John 2:2; 4:10).

And finally, it was a reconciling death. When a husband and wife fuss and go so far as to dislike one another, what they need is a counselor to reconcile them—or put them back together. When Adam and Eve sinned, they turned their back on God and because of their sin, God had to turn His back on the human race. But the death of Jesus reconciled God and man. "God was in Christ reconciling the world to Himself" (2 Cor. 5:19).

Think about It

Question: What do you know about the death of famous people? What death has influenced the world more than the death of Jesus Christ? Besides the redemptive factor, what benefits have spread to humankind because of Christ's death?

Answer: Those whose lives have been transformed by Christ's death have been motivated to tell others so they too can experience the benefits of His death. As a matter of fact, they have sacrificed their time and pleasures to tell everyone, "Christ died for you and He has a wonderful plan for your life."

4

CHRISTIANITY IS A MIRACULOUS RESURRECTION

There are many world religions, but none of them makes the claim that its founder rose from the dead as does Christianity. Buddha, the founder of Buddhism, lived, died, and left behind a religion of 300–400 million followers worldwide. But his body is still in the grave. Nowhere in his literature or among his followers have they claimed that he has been raised from the dead. The same is true with Confucius, Muhammad, and all the other founders of religions. All died, and they remain in the grave.

Christianity is the only world religion to claim that its founder not only died, but bodily rose again. When the women arrived at the tomb on Easter Sunday morning, an angel said to them, "I know that you seek Jesus who was crucified. He is not here; for He is risen, as He said. Come see the place where the Lord lay. And go quickly and tell his disciples that He is risen from the dead" (Matt. 28:5–7).

The question of life after death has been an age-old inquiry. Job said, "If a man dies, shall he live again?" (Job 14:14).

The opponents of Christianity almost always concentrate their attacks on the resurrection because if they can invalidate Jesus' resurrection, then all the other claims of Christianity collapse. If there is no resurrection, then there is no Christianity.

Because of the perfect life of Jesus Christ, one should have expected something unusual about His death. Jesus was not just any man; He was the God-Man. He told his followers, "He who has seen me has seen the Father" (John 14:9). And "I and my Father are one" (John 10:30). The Jews surely understood Jesus claimed deity, for they told Pilate, "He ought to die because He made himself the son of God" (John 19:7). Can God be kept in a grave?

Jesus' perfect life, His God-like character, His powerful miracles, and His lofty sermons would be anti-climatic, if there were not a continuation after death and no sequel to his life.

Therefore, considering all that Jesus was, one might expect a resurrection after His death. But Jesus was more than ordinary man—He was God. Since life is one of the characteristics of God, He could not be kept in the grave. And given that Jesus said, "I am the resurrection" (John 11:25), Jesus' resurrection is the fulfillment of His pronouncement.

The book of Acts would have never happened if there were no resurrection. Individuals may follow a great dead leader as long as their memories endure. But after a while, dedication to a dead leader diminishes. And with time, people tend to forget about him altogether. But the resurrection is proved by the fact that Christians not only remember

Jesus, they get bolder in their ministry and more successful based on the power of a resurrected Christ in them.

Jesus was a leader who taught that right would prevail over wrong, and if there were no resurrection, all the vicious acts of the Jews and Roman soldiers would have prevailed.

The Proofs of Resurrection

The resurrection is proved by the phenomenon of the empty tomb. The casual observer should have realized that something supernatural happened in the tomb. The Jewish leaders who manipulated Rome to crucify Jesus remembered Jesus claimed that He would rise again. So they went to Pilate and got him to assign Roman soldiers to guard the tomb. The Jewish leaders didn't want the followers of Jesus to steal the body, and then claim He had been raised from the dead. When the angel rolled the stone from the tomb entrance, the soldiers ran away.

On Easter Sunday morning, a group of women came early to the tomb, and an angel invited them to look inside the empty tomb. "He is not here; for He has risen, as He said. Come, see the place where the Lord lay" (Matt. 28:6). Later that morning John and Peter came to the tomb and "saw the linen cloths lying there, and the handkerchief that had been around His head, not lying with the linen cloths, but folded together in a place by itself" (John 20:6–7). They didn't see a body.

Later on in the morning Mary Magdalene came to the empty tomb where she met a man. Mary didn't recognize the man who asked, "Woman, why are you weeping?" (John 20:15). Mary thought he was the gardener, so she volunteered, "Sir, if you have carried Him away, tell me where you have laid Him, and I will take Him away" (John 20:15). She didn't know that the resurrected Christ was speaking to her until He spoke her name, "Mary." All she could respond was "Rabboni!"

Joseph of Arimathea and Nicodemus brought approximately one hundred pounds of myrrh and aloes to anoint the corpse of Jesus (John 19:36). This is equivalent to a very large bucket of cream, similar to hand lotion. "They took the body of Jesus, and bound it in strips of linen with the spices" (John 19:40). As they wrapped these long strips of cloth around the body of Jesus, they poured on the lotion forming a shell, something like an old-fashioned cast that is put on a broken leg. As the cream dried, it bonded with the linen cloth making it impossible to unwrap without destroying the plaster cast. When John saw the linen cloths lying and the handkerchief at another place, "He saw and believed" (John 20:8). John was the first disciple to believe in the physical resurrection of Jesus Christ.

The sudden transformation of frightened disciples into bold proponents of the resurrection is another proof of the resurrection. All the disciples, except for John, had run away and hidden when Jesus was arrested and crucified. But the scared disciples were transformed when they saw Jesus Christ because, "He showed them His hands and His side" (John 20:20). Or as one nineteenth-century author stated:

> It is astonishing that a few simple and uneducated men should have been able to devise and execute a plan, which has eluded all search, and has obtained credit among the wise and learned, as well as among the vulgar, for the space of eighteen hundred years.[7]

The resurrection is proved by the rapid emergence of the church, which is a fellowship of like believers claiming to be the body of Christ in whose midst He lived and empowered them for godliness and service. If Jesus had not been raised from the dead, how could this group have become worldwide in their influence? Notice what the enemies said about the early church, "These who have turned the world upside down have come here too" (Acts 17:6).

The resurrection of Christ is proved by the testimony of various individuals and groups of people who claimed they talked with and had fellowship with the resurrected Christ. First, a group of women leaving the tomb met Jesus and worshipped Him (Matt. 28:9–10). Second, Mary Magdalene met Him at the tomb: "Mary Magdalene came and told the disciples that she had seen the Lord, and that He had spoken these things to her" (John 20:18). Then on Easter Sunday evening, Jesus met ten disciples in an upper room (John 20:19–23) and a week later, He met eleven disciples in the same upper room (Mark 16:14). This is when He invited Thomas to " 'Reach your finger here, and look at My hands; and reach your hand here, and put it into My side. Do not be unbelieving, but believing.' And Thomas answered and said to Him, 'My Lord and my God!' Jesus said to him, 'Thomas, because you have seen Me, you have believed. Blessed are those who have not seen and yet have believed' " (John 20:27–29). Jesus also appeared privately to Peter and to James (His half brother). Still later Jesus appeared to five hundred people. These various appearances of Jesus coincide with the credibility of testimony needed in a court room, that is, consistency, reliability, and repeatability.

The physical resurrection is proved by the transformation of Paul, a Christ-hating persecutor of Christians into a fervent preacher of the gospel. Paul was heading to Damascus to arrest Christians when he met Jesus Christ near the city gate (Acts 9). Paul was changed by that encounter, and became the bold witness to the Gentiles throughout the Mediterranean world.

The resurrection of Jesus Christ is proved by the testimony of believers in whom Christ dwelt. Perhaps the greatest testimony is Paul who said, "I have been crucified with Christ; it is no longer I who live, but Christ lives in me . . ." (Gal. 2:20). Many have become Christians as a result of placing their faith in Christ. Then at this point, Christ comes to live in their life (Col. 1:28) and the presence of Jesus Christ in their life becomes the transforming power for each Christian to live for God.

The resurrection is proved by the New Testament, which completely and historically explains the doctrine of the resurrection of Jesus Christ. Every one of the twenty-seven books of the New Testament is based on the physical resurrection of Jesus Christ. If Christ did not rise from the dead, then the historical accuracy of each of the New Testament books can be questioned. Each of these authors wrote apart from one another, and yet their view of the resurrection remains consistent. This again points to the credibility that Jesus, in fact, did rise from the dead.

The resurrection is proved by the inability of the Jewish leaders to disprove that Jesus arose from the dead, in the very city where He died and was buried. As has already been said, these Jewish leaders heard Jesus say that He would rise from the dead. And they did everything they could to make sure that His body was not stolen. When the angel appeared to roll away the stone, "The guards shook for fear of him, and became like dead men" (Matt. 28:4).

What did the guards do? "Some of the guard came into the city and reported to the chief priests all the things that had happened. When they had assembled with the elders and consulted together, they gave a large sum of money to the soldiers, saying, "Tell them, 'His disciples came at night and stole Him away while we slept.' And if this comes to the governor's ears, we will appease him and make you secure" (Matt. 28:11–14).

The physical resurrection is proved by the change in the day of worship from Saturday to Sunday. This was a monumental shift of attitude. Ever since the Ten Commandments had been given 1,400 years earlier, the Jews had worshipped on the Sabbath, the last day of the week. The Jews were so entrenched in Sabbath-keeping, they wanted to kill Jesus when He broke their man-made laws. But when thousands of Jews became followers of Jesus, they wanted to worship on the day Jesus arose from the dead, that is, the first day of the week. Sunday suddenly became the universally observed day of worship. A new law or commandment by earthly leaders could have never changed the attitude of the people to worship on a different day from Saturday. But when Jesus entered the hearts of Christians, they wanted to worship Him on the most important day of Christianity— the day He arose from the dead.

The resurrection is evidenced by the conversion of James, the half brother of Christ. Paul mentions that after the resurrection, "He (Jesus) was seen of James, then of all the apostles" (1 Cor. 15:7). Wouldn't a brother recognize a hoax? Apparently James was an unbeliever until the resurrected Jesus appeared to him (John 7:5).

The resurrection is proved by the testimony of Ignatius of Antioch, who was born about AD 30, when Jesus was raised from the dead. Ignatius was later martyred by Emperor Trajan (AD 97–117) when he was thrown to the beasts in the Flavian amphitheatre in Rome. Ignatius wrote:

> As for me, I know that even after His resurrection He was in the flesh, and I believe this to be true. For, when He came to those who were with Peter, He said to them: "Take hold on me and handle and see that I am not a spirit without a body." And, as soon as they touched Him and felt His flesh and pulse, they believed. It is for this reason that they despised death and even showed themselves superior to death. After His resurrection He ate and drank with them like anyone else with a body, although in His spirit He was one with the Father. (Ignatius of Antioch, Epistle to the Smyrnaeans, chapter 3, reprinted in Francis Glimm, *The Apostolic Fathers* (Washington, DC: The Catholic University of America Press, 1962), 119.[8]

The Essence of the Resurrection

When Jesus was raised from the dead, it certified what He had accomplished in His death. Notice Paul wrote that Christ "was delivered over to death for our sins and was raised to life for our justification" (Rom 4:25, NIV). Whereas the death of Jesus forgave us our sins, it was the resurrection that gave us new life and a perfect standing with God.

Also, His resurrection vindicated what Jesus predicted. In a confrontation with the Jews Jesus said, "Destroy this temple, and in three days I will raise it up" (John 2:19). The Jews thought He was speaking about Herod's Temple but Jesus was referring to the temple of His body. "When He had risen from the dead, His disciples remembered that He had said this to them; and they believed the Scripture and the word which Jesus had said" (John 2:22).

If Jesus had stayed in the grave, it would have denied what He said, "I am the resurrection" (John 11:25). But His physical resurrection validated His description that He was both resurrection and life.

The resurrection was more than an event to the early church; it was the focal point of their preaching. One criterion for an apostle to take Judas' place was his ability "to become a witness with us of His resurrection" (Acts 1:22). The message of this resurrection was to give authority to their preaching, "And with great power the apostles gave witness to the resurrection of the Lord Jesus" (Acts 4:33).

Source of Spiritual Transformation

Jesus was not alone when He came out of the grave. The Bible teaches that believers were in Christ when the Savior died, and they were also in Him when He was raised again. Paul says, "But God . . . raised us up together, and made us sit together in the heavenly places in Christ Jesus" (Eph. 2:4–6). The transforming truth of this passage is that every believer is "in Christ Jesus." Jesus had promised this unique identity the night before He died when He said, "You in Me, and I in you" (John 14:20).

For that reason, all that Jesus received in the resurrection, Christians also receive. Jesus received new life to His old corpse, and in Jesus Christ believers receive new life. Because of Jesus' resurrection, He has ascended into heaven and believers also are in Jesus in both the ascension and His glorified seat in heaven.

Technically, the believer lives in two worlds. He lives "in the heavenlies" (Eph 1:3). This is the new position a Christian has "in Christ." The believer also lives on this earth with all its limitations, temptations, and decay. Therefore, the believer, who is living "in Christ" in the heavenlies, has a new authority to overcome the temptations of this life.

Because believers are "in Christ," they have new power to live victoriously for God. Paul had said, "That I may know Him and the power of His resurrection" (Phil 3:10). The power that Christ had to overcome death is the same power Christians have to victoriously overcome sin and the problems of this world.

The resurrection is the basis for all believers' assurance of salvation. Christians can know they have eternal life because Christ was raised from the dead to give it to them. "And if Christ is not risen, then our preaching is empty and your faith is also empty" (1 Cor. 15:14). What does that mean? It means that if there is no resurrection, then there is no forgiveness of sins.

And if there is no resurrection, what about all those Christians who believed in the death, burial, and resurrection of Jesus Christ and yet, they died? Where are they today? "And if Christ is not risen . . . . Then also those who have fallen asleep in Christ have perished" (1 Cor. 15:17–18).

Think about It

Question: What is the greatest proof of the resurrection?

Answer: There are several proofs for the resurrection given in this chapter, each one strong enough to stand by itself. But the greatest proof is the presence of the indwelling Christ in your heart. Since you can't lie to yourself, and only you can correctly know your own inward experience, then the indwelling presence of Jesus Christ is your absolute assurance that He arose from the grave.

5

✦

CHRISTIANITY IS A LIFE-TRANSFORMING EXPERIENCE

Before I was saved, I picked up the bad habit of cursing. When I was about nine years old, I went to our church's Presbyterian Youth Fellowship. One evening, as we met, there was a candle on the table in front of the young people and a small bowl. We were given a small piece of paper and a pencil, and told to write our sins on the sheet of paper. I wrote the word *cursing*, crumpled the paper up, and put it in the bowl. When the leader touched the candle to all the crumpled pieces of paper, I inwardly thought, *God, there goes my cursing up in flames.* But I found that cursing came back.

Approximately two months later, we had the same ceremony. Except this time I didn't write the word *cursing* on my sheet of paper. I wrote down several of the actual curse words. I thought this was a great act of repentance. And when they were burned up, I again said, "God, there goes my cursing." But bad words came back.

In high school I went to the Presbyterian camp and on the last night during the bonfire service, several young people went forward, took a small chip of wood, gave a testimony, and threw their chip into the fire. I was so moved that I picked up a chip of wood that had been splattered by dirt. I held it high for everyone to see and said, "This chip of wood represents my dirty tongue." Then I made a great statement of repentance, "I will no longer curse." As I threw my chip into the fire, I was deeply committed to keep my speech pure.

I kept my commitment for approximately two weeks, until something happened for which I was not prepared. The newspapers I was delivering every afternoon came bundled with wire. As I bent the wire back and forth to break it, suddenly a jagged end popped loose and gashed my knuckle. Blood gushed out, and I cursed the paper. My good friend Art Winn reminded me that I had promised to never curse again, so I cursed him. I came to the conclusion that I couldn't give up my sin, so I never again tried to quit cursing.

On July 25, 1950, I met Jesus Christ. When I did, I didn't just repent of my cursing. I was sorry for all my sin. I asked Jesus to come into my life. He did, and He transformed me, including my speech. Out of that experience, I never cursed again.

Just because children are born into a family of Christians does not make them a Christian. Everyone who becomes a Christian has made a decision to follow Jesus Christ. Those who embrace Christ as their Lord and Savior are transformed through the process that's called *conversion*. This means they turn from sin (repentance) to complete dependence (faith) upon Christ to save them.

Conversion is one of the most misunderstood of all religious terms. It's a human term, something that people do. Years ago, Elizabeth Taylor married Eddie Fisher, who was Jewish, so she converted to the Jewish faith. Cassius Clay was heavyweight champion of the world when he converted to the Muslim faith. According to the dictionary, conversion is being changed from one use to another.[9]

In the football world, a conversion is the extra point(s) after a touchdown. In mathematics, conversion is the reduction of a mathematical expression by clearing of fractions. A religious conversion is the decision to adopt a religion. In essence, everyone who adopts a religion is converted to that religion whether it be Buddhist, Confucianism, or Bahá'í.

According to the Bible, conversion is a voluntary change of the mind, emotions, and will by the sinner, as the person turns from sin to Christ as Savior. In summary, conversion is what a person does by turning to Christ.

One Door—Two Sides

But think of conversion as a door with two sides. On one side of the door is the term *human activity*, and on the other side of the door is *God's activity*. A human makes a decision to convert, that's when he pushes on the door into heaven. On the other side of the door is God's action, which is regeneration; the convert is born again, or given new life. When a person meets God's criteria for conversion, God gives him eternal life and a new nature. Then he becomes a child of God.

There are three parts to the conversion experience. First, there is intellect. A person must know that he is a sinner, "For all have sinned and fall short of the glory of God"

(Rom. 3:23). That means they know they are under the condemnation of God because of their sin, "For the wages of sin is death" (Rom. 6:23). Then, the person must know that Christ has suffered for his sins. "Christ died for us" (Rom. 5:8). Knowing all these facts does not save anyone; this does not push the door open into heaven. Jesus said, "Not everyone who says to Me, 'Lord, Lord,' shall enter the kingdom of heaven, but he who does the will of My Father in heaven" (Matt. 7:21). An individual doesn't become a Christian simply by learning about Christ, nor does one become a Christian by following a set of rules.

The second part of conversion is emotions. Paul describes the emotional distress of the Corinthians: "Your sorrow led to repentance" (2 Cor. 7:9). These emotions are reflective of a heart that wants to be converted. Paul continued to describe their conversion, "For godly sorrow produces repentance leading to salvation" (2 Cor. 7:10). However, just because one weeps does not mean that person has given his life to Christ. Paul describes those who sorrow but were not converted, "The sorrow of the world produces death" (2 Cor. 7:10).

The third part of conversion is the decision whereby the individual chooses God. One aspect of choice is repentance, where Peter said, "Repent therefore and be converted" (Acts 3:19). This described the action of the will, "If anyone desires to come after Me, let him deny himself, and take up his cross daily, and follow Me" (Luke 9:23).

What do these three functions of the personality mean? No one is saved by knowledge alone, emotions alone, or by a choice alone. Rather, conversion is based on a correct knowledge of the Word of God that Jesus has died for one's sins and has been raised to give new life (intellect).

Then, the human heart must experience a conviction for sin and have an overwhelming love for God (emotions). Finally, based on correct knowledge and feeling, the person must choose to accept Jesus Christ as his Savior (will).

Earlier I said that simply knowing about Jesus Christ doesn't save a person. And neither does remorse over sin save a person, nor keeping the rules of a church save an individual.

But making Jesus Christ an intimate part of your life makes you a Christian.

The Faith Experience

Conversion is the psychological explanation of what a person does when they exercise faith in God. Faith is absolutely imperative for salvation, "For by grace you have been saved through faith" (Eph. 2:8).

Faith is simple, yet at the same time complex. Faith is as simple and quick as a drowning man reaching for a rope. When the dying thief asked Jesus, "Remember me Lord, remember me when You come into Your kingdom" (Luke 23:42), immediately his faith saved him. Jesus said, "Today you will be with Me in Paradise" (Luke 23:43).

Yet, faith is as complex as is the total inner person, which uses all one's faculties to reach out to God. Just as conversion involves the total personality, so faith involves the total inner person putting all one's trust in God.

Faith is more than knowing about God. If knowing about God is all it took, the devils would be saved, but they are not. "The devils believe—and tremble!" (James 2:19).

Faith is not doing something for God. Jesus said, "Many will say to Me in that day, 'Lord, Lord, have we not prophesied in Your name . . . and done many wonders in Your name?' " (Matt. 7:22). But Jesus will answer them, "I never knew you" (Matt. 7:23).

Don't try to make faith too hard. Paul was beaten for a crime he didn't commit and was imprisoned in the middle of the night. God sent an earthquake that opened the doors and unlocked the shackles that held the prisoners. The Philippian jailer ran in, thinking his prisoners had escaped, and was ready to kill himself. Paul told him to stop. It's then that the jailer asked the eternal question, "What must I do to be saved?" (Acts 16:30). The answer was very simple, "Believe on the Lord Jesus Christ, and you will be saved" (Acts 16:31).

The Philippian jailer was ready to commit suicide but Paul stopped him. Paul didn't have to tell him to repent, nor did Paul have to tell him to trust God with all his heart. The Philippian jailer had already done that. All Paul said was "believe." It was as simple as that!

Saving faith is when the total inner person believes Jesus died for him. When the Ethiopian eunuch wanted Christian baptism, Philip gave one criterion for baptism: "If you believe with all your heart" (Acts 8:37). Obviously, to believe "with all your heart" meant every part of his inner being.

The Bible is a source for one's faith. Because the Bible is God's Word, then God gets into the heart of a man through the Scriptures. God convicts a person of sin and convinces him that Jesus has died for his sin. "Faith comes . . . by the word of God" (Rom. 10:17). Because the Bible is supernatural, when a person reads and believes it, faith begins to grow within the heart. Because the Bible promises eternal life, when a person reads and believes it, he acts on the promises of eternal life.

The Born Again Experience (Regeneration)

Remember the door we looked at earlier. The human side of the door is called conversion, and the divine side of the door is called regeneration. When an individual is regenerated, that person is born again. *Regeneration* and *born again* are two terms used interchangeably.

Nicodemus was a wealthy religious teacher who came to Jesus by night. Jesus told him, "Most assuredly, I say to you, unless one is born again, he cannot see the kingdom of God" (John 3:3). Nicodemus had one of the best educations in Jerusalem, but it was not enough. Nicodemus also served God as a religious leader, but that was not enough. Nicodemus had an apparent holy life, but that was not enough. Nicodemus had to be born again. To be regenerated, or born again, means a change of the heart, wrought by the Holy Spirit, who gives a person eternal life and a predisposition to do God's will.

While conversion is what a person does, regeneration is what God does. God regenerates a person through the Holy Spirit when an individual is "born of the Spirit" (John 3:6).

How does one experience the new birth? It's very simple: "Whoever believes that Jesus is the Christ is born of God" (1 John 5:1). An individual is born again by believing and receiving Christ as Savior. "As many as received Him [Christ] . . . were born of God" (John 1:12–13).

When a person is born again, he receives a new nature that wants to serve God. The Bible says, "We know that whoever is born of God does not sin; but he who has been born of God keeps himself, and the wicked one does not touch him" (1 John 5:18). Don't get upset by that phrase "does not sin." At another place the Scriptures say that every Christian sins (1 John 1:8–10). This phrase "does not sin" literally means "does not sin continually."

When you're born again, personally, you have a new nature that wants to serve God, but you still have the old nature. You're still tempted to do wrong. The issue always is, "What will you choose?" Will you give in to the old nature to sin, or will you follow the new nature and choose not to sin?

Think about It

Question: What is the greatest proof that Christianity is real to those who have never read the Scripture or heard a sermon?

Answer: The changed life of a Christian is the only way that most unbelieving people will encounter Christianity. They will probably not read the Bible or hear a sermon. Paul told the Thessalonians, "You became examples to all in Macedonia and Achaia . . . Your faith toward God has gone out, so that we do not need to say anything" (1 Thess. 1:7–8). Therefore, your life can become an effective testimony to those people you see everyday.

6

CHRISTIANITY IS AN ONGOING RELATIONSHIP WITH GOD

Every religion teaches that its adherents can relate to their deity. Christianity is no different, but the relationship that a Christian has with God is vastly different from the other empty religions of the world.

Examine briefly how some religions expect their adherents to relate to the Supreme Being. The Muslim expresses absolute obedience to Allah, even to the point of blowing himself up as a suicide bomber. But the Muslim doesn't believe he can have a personal relationship with Allah because he doesn't believe Allah has personality.

The Buddhist gives hours to contemplation and meditation with a view of emptying himself so he can be rid of the sorrows of life.

The Hindu religion emphasizes dharma (the worshipper's duty is fulfilled by observing social customs or law) resulting in mystical contemplation and ascetic practices.

The Christian meditates on Scripture and on the person of Christ to fill himself with the knowledge of Christ.

Christianity offers the Christian a relationship with God that has practical implications in this world. The indwelling Christ gives the believer love for his fellow man, peace in the troubled world, and purpose in life. The indwelling Christ helps a Christian overcome his weaknesses and gives him great ambitions to do exploits for God.

It Begins with Jesus

The night before He died, Jesus set the stage for His continuing relationship with His followers. He told them, "I shall be with you a little while longer . . . where I am going, you cannot [immediately] come" (John 13:33). Then Jesus explained, "No, I will not abandon you as orphans—I will come to you" (John 14:18, NLT).

That night Jesus explained a unique relationship they would have with Him, "You in Me, and I in you" (John 14:20). Jesus told His followers they would be in Him, meaning their life would be identified with Christ. But the second aspect of that relationship was "I in you." This means Christ would indwell them. To become a Christian a person invites Christ to live in his life (John 1:12). At that point Christ lives in the individual—the indwelling life— to help believers in their Christian practice and Christian walk.

Did you see the word "orphans" in the above verse? An orphan doesn't have anyone to protect him or look after his needs. Jesus was promising Christians they would not have to live and minister by themselves, but that He would come to them in their storms to meet their needs and provide for them. This intimate relationship between Christ and His followers is a unique feature of Christianity.

Prayer Relationship

The first relationship is connecting to God by prayer. When Jesus left He said, "You haven't done this before. Ask, using my name, and you will receive, and you will have abundant joy" (John 16:24, NLT). Jesus was promising His followers they could have a prayer-relationship with God the Father by praying in His name. Jesus explained, "You will ask the Father directly, and he will grant your request because you use my name" (John 16:23, NLT).

At another place, Jesus told His followers, "Men always ought to pray and not lose heart" (Luke 18:1). The word for *prayer* in this verse is *proseuchamai*. It comes from two words—*pros* meaning toward and *euchamai* meaning the face. This defines prayer as a face-to-face relationship with God. *Proseuchamai* is the most used word for prayer in the New Testament, suggesting that Christians should have intimate conversations with God. Hence, prayer is not just asking for things, but rather prayer is talking to God and enjoying an intimate relationship with Him.

There are many different ways for Christians to relate to God in prayer—intercession for others, request for needs, praise and adoration to God, meditative prayer (thinking of God), warfare prayer against spiritual enemies, repentance after sinning, prayer of blessing others, and the prayer of faith for physical healing.[10]

I must also mention "praying the Lord's Prayer." When I use the Lord's Prayer, I cover every area to petition that I need to pray. The Lord's Prayer contains everything a Christian must know and every way that a Christian must pray. Christians should pray this prayer every day.[11]

Worship is perhaps the most intimate of all the ongoing relationships with God. It is something that God wants for every Christian. Jesus told the woman at the well, "The Father is looking for those who will worship him" (John 4:23, NLT). Why is the Father looking for worship? Because this is the one thing that God cannot do for Himself. God can't worship Himself. Since meaningful worship comes from the heart, God wants His followers to worship and praise Him from their hearts. Jesus finished the above conversation with the woman saying, "These who worship Him, must worship God from the depths of their heart according to patterns taught in Scripture" (John 4:24, author translation).

Living in Two Worlds

The believer actually lives in this present, evil world, but he also lives in a heavenly world. The earthly world is filled with temptation, failure, sickness, and sorrow. In the heavenly world, the believer enjoys all the blessings that Christ makes available to him. The standard is that a believer should conduct his life in this earthly world by the principles God has bestowed upon him in the heavenly world. Also, the promises of the heavenly world should motivate the believer to sacrifice for Christ in this present world, knowing what is available in the next world.

More than 150 times in the New Testament the believer is described as being "in Christ." What does that mean? When Jesus said "you in Me" (John 14:20), He meant a believer should look at all the benefits promised to him "in the heavenlies."[12] The believer is chosen in Christ (Eph. 1:4) and adopted like a child (Eph. 1:5). In salvation the believer dies in Christ, but is then made alive in Christ (Eph 2:5), and God "raised us up together, and made us sit together in the heavenly places in Christ Jesus" (Eph. 2:6). All of this means that the believer is promised a heavenly view.

Because the believer is "in Christ," then "in the ages to come He might show the exceeding riches of His grace in His kindness toward us in Christ Jesus" (Eph. 2:7). Christians are not perfect in this world, but "in Christ" they stand perfect before the Father's throne. They have the righteousness of Christ (2 Cor. 5:21). Since the Christian has this wonderful position in Christ, he needs to conform his daily, earthly life to heavenly standards.

The earthly world in which Christians live is filled with evil, trials, and failure. Christians will face temptation (James 1:12–13) and sometimes they will yield to it and fall into sin (1 John 1:8, 10). Christians do not live perfect lives in this imperfect world. They need to repent, confess their sins (1 John 1:9), and come back to God. Christians do try their best, but they fail.

Satan is alive and well in the world, and the devil loves to confound Christians, defeat their projects, and persecute them. Jesus reminds His followers, "If they persecuted Me, they will also persecute you" (John 15:20). But the Christian has a present hope in the evil world. Jesus promised, "I [am] in you" (John 14:20). The second half of living in two worlds is that Christ lives in the Christian. He gives them courage to face dangers; He gives strength to overcome trials; He gives inward peace in the midst of storms; and He gives constant inner assurance to His followers that they belong to Him—that they are part of His plan for the world.

They have the abiding promise of "Christ in you, the hope of glory" (Col. 1:27).

Special Encounters

There are special times in a believer's relationship with God that God meets with His followers in a special way. I have called these *epochs*, defined by the dictionary as "an event or a time marked by an event that begins a new period or development; a memorable event or date."[13]

This special time occurs:

1. When one intentionally meets with God
2. In a time of great personal need
3. When God meets with someone through unexpected circumstances
4. When God reveals something of Himself
5. When a person has an intimate contact with God
6. When a believer prepares for a specific task
7. When the person probably doesn't fully understand all the mysterious elements of the encounter

- *Intentionally.* Some encounters are initiated by God when the Christian least expects it. At other times, God comes to an individual when he is so fervent in prayer that he won't back off. Jacob wrestled with God all night, refusing to release his wrestling hold on God. God heard Jacob and changed his life (Gen. 32:24–28). Moses would not let God send an angel to guide him into the Promised Land. He said in faith, "If Your Presence does not go with us, do not bring us up from here" (Ex. 33:15).

- *Time of great need.* When backslidden and discouraged, Elijah experienced a turnaround when he met God. Jeremiah, Isaiah, and Ezekiel encountered God when they saw their nation collapsing around them. Huge problems motivated these men to search for God, while others encountered God, even when they were in rebellion against Him. Paul hated Jesus when Christ met him on the Damascus road to transform his life. Peter had denied Jesus three times, so Jesus met the fisherman on the shore of Lake Galilee to ask, "Do you love Me?" The wonderful thing about these encounters is that when people needed God, He came to them.

- *Surprising encounter.* Some in Scripture did not expect to encounter God. Mary came to the garden to anoint a corpse but ended up talking to a living Christ. Others, such as Abraham, prayed for God to bless them and were surprised by the magnitude of God's response.

- *A message from God.* When God encounters an individual, He has a purpose in doing so. Usually God has a particular message to give or a task to do. Jesus appeared to the apostle John on the isle of Patmos. He wanted John to write the book of Revelation. It was a simple, straightforward task: "Write the things which you have seen, and the things which are, and the things which will take place after this" (Rev. 1:19). While God does not speak audibly today, when a person meets God He does impress on his heart what He wants him to know.

- *Knowing God intimately.* God wants an individual to know Him intimately. He encounters a person so that he will meet with Him and know Him better. Doesn't He say, "Be still, and know that I am God"? (Ps 46:10).

Paul obviously met Christ and learned of Him when he met the Savior on the Damascus road. Yet at the end of his life, Paul's desire was, "That I may know Him and the power of His resurrection" (Phil. 3:10).

- *Changing encounters.* After a Christian encounters God in a special epoch, he will be different. Meeting with God will change a person's life. Moses' face shone. Abraham received a son. Paul was called to ministry. Peter was given a new commission for ministry. Those who meet with God have their life changed.

- *Mysterious elements of the encounter.* There are many things about a relationship with God that a believer will not understand. He doesn't understand everything about the infinity of God because he is a finite human. There is usually something mysterious in the ways God does things. A Christian still has a sin nature that blinds him spiritually to some of the things happening around him. Paul states, "We now see in a mirror, dimly, but then face to face. Now I know in part, but then I shall know just as I also am known" (1 Cor. 13:12). There is a mystery in every encounter with God. Perhaps God doesn't explain everything that's happening around you because He is testing your faith. He wants to know if you will trust and obey Him. He wants you to bow before Him in worship.

Think about It

I have a pastor friend in the Episcopal Church who offers an unusual invocation at the beginning of his worship services. You will appreciate his prayer after reading this chapter. He greets his congregation with uplifted hands and says, *"Today you can touch God . . . right here . . . right now . . . you can enter His presence and touch God."*

Then my Episcopalian friend smiles at the congregation and offers them the greatest hope any pastor ever promised a congregation, *"But more importantly than your touching God . . . God can touch you."*

7

CHRISTIANITY IS A DISCIPLINED LIFESTYLE

While in high school my buddy, Art Winn, and I went squirrel hunting. We were walking in the bottom of a twelve-foot drainage ditch when the ditch forked in two directions. The two branches surrounded a farmer's field and met about one mile ahead. Art took the right branch and I took the left. After he left it began to rain, and I crawled under the overhanging root system of an oak tree, which gave me a cavelike protection.

I lay in the dry leaves for several minutes before realizing how cold I was. Pulling some leaves together, I made a fire. In the light of the flames, I saw a huge black snake lying right beside me. I enjoyed the cave until the light revealed the snake; that's when I scrambled out of the cave. No way was I going to go back, not even to get out of the rain.

The same thing happens in the Christian life. A Christian may be comfortable with sin in his life until the light of Christ reveals their true nature. The sin may be as dangerous as a snake, or the sin simply may make the Christian uncomfortable in his present situation. In either case, the Christian should begin to live differently because of his salvation.

Jesus noted the changes He expected in followers: "If anyone desires to come after Me, let him deny himself, and take up his cross daily, and follow Me" (Luke 9:23). Self-denial is the first step of a disciplined life.

In one sense, salvation transforms the inner person, but Jesus expects the new convert to discipline his outward life to conform to His expectations. Paul explains what God expects, "I plead with you to give your bodies to God. Let them be a living sacrifice—the kind he will accept. When you think of what he has done for you, is this too much to ask? Don't copy the behavior and customs of this world, but be a new and different person with a fresh newness in all you do and think" (Rom. 12:1–2, TLB).

Why must a person exercise self-discipline? Jesus explains that the old nature desires all types of evil, "For out of the heart proceed evil thoughts, murders, adulteries, fornications, thefts, false witness, blasphemies. These are the things which defile a man" (Matt. 15:19–20). For that reason, the Christian must use all diligence to discipline himself not to give in to sin or his old nature.

In view of this, the Christian must form good habits that please God and lead to godliness. Paul states that Christians should "deny ungodliness and worldly lusts, we should live soberly, righteously, and godly in the present age" (Titus 2:12).

The following principles are those that guide Christians in disciplining their lifestyle.

1. *Christians must discipline themselves to do what God directs.* The Westminster Confession of Faith asks the question, "What is sin?" The first part of the answer is, "Sin is

any want of conformity unto . . . the law of God."[14] Anything that does not conform to God's Word is sin.

When a mother says to her son, "Go to the store and get bread," she expects him to obey. What should be her reaction when she finds him playing baseball on the corner? She can't be happy. In the same way God expects Christians to develop their inner life by praying (John 14:13–14), by studying the Scriptures (2 Tim. 2:15), and by witnessing to unbelievers (Acts 1:8), plus many other commands that involve developing a positive, healthy attitude.

Within the corporate church life, Christians are to tithe (Mal. 3:10), attend worship services (Heb. 10:25), and love other Christians (John 13:34). These are but a few of the areas where Christians must form outward habits of obedience. The Scriptures teach, "Therefore, to him who knows to do good and does not do it, to him it is sin" (James 4:17).

2. Christians must discipline themselves to refrain from doing what God says is wrong. The Ten Commandments are negative warnings beginning, "Thou shalt not . . ." When Christians go against God's commandments, they not only sin but develop habits that will bring outward harm to their lives. God says it is wrong to kill, lie, steal, commit adultery, and have idols in one's life (Ex. 20:3–17).

The commands of God are not grievous; He did not take away the "fun" things. Many mistakenly think, *All pleasures are gone now that I am a Christian.* God is not an angry father who keeps His children from having fun. Jesus said, "I have come that they may have life, and that they may have it more abundantly" (John 10:10).

But like a wise father, God knows that some things will harm His children. What parents would allow their children to play near a busy highway or in a field with snakes? When

God says "no," a Christian should not rebel or see how close he can get to the edge. When a Christian understands the purpose of God is to keep him safe, he can obey with enthusiasm.

3. *Christians must discipline themselves to obey their conscience.* The conscience is a moral regulator that flashes information to the brain. It informs what it thinks is right and wrong. Like a thermostat in the house, when things get chilly, the furnace starts up. When the conscience notifies Christians that something is wrong, it is dangerous to go against it. At birth, the conscience is pure, reflecting the standards of God in whose image individuals were made. The conscience informs a person that it's wrong to murder, steal, cuss, and lie. The conscience is God's moral law branded in the heart.

I grew up with an alcoholic father and saw the misery he caused my mother. Our family had to do without because he drank so heavily. I don't know if a person becomes an alcoholic by outward influence or physical traits passed from parent to child, but I've always had a fear of liquor of any kind. I was afraid I might become an alcoholic.

I once refused Communion because real wine was served. To this day, I will not eat meat cooked in liquor, even though people tell me the alcohol is boiled off. My conscience tells me if I got one taste, I could become an alcoholic. Some may think I am narrow, but I try to let my conscience be my guide. "If someone thinks that a particular food (or drink) is unclean, then it is unclean for him" (Rom. 14:14, author translation).

While I feel it's a sin to ignore the conscience, I also know that the conscience cannot always be trusted. A person's conscience can be "seared" to think that wrong is right, or visa versa. "Having their own conscience seared with a hot iron" (1 Timothy 4:2). This pictures a scab on the skin as the result of a hot poker burn. The conscience can be seared when one continually goes against its instructions.

First, not everything that the conscience allows may be right. Some people think it's allowable to steal or lie under certain conditions. Second, the conscience won't notify a person of every event that is wrong. The conscience depends upon the training it has received. Some people commit adultery not realizing what God has said about sexual purity. Third, it's wrong for an individual to go against one's conscience, even when others disagree. Christians want to live with a pure conscience, meaning that they want to live peaceably with themselves. They have disciplined their conscience to think right, and have disciplined their actions to follow the dictates of their conscience.

4. *Christians must discipline their thought life so they don't harbor impure thought.* Visual temptations are everywhere. Men enjoy thumbing through *Playboy* or walking the beaches to look at the bikinis. Some wives understand this and say, "It's all right to window shop; just don't touch." Yet, even in this "body watcher" age, Christians are to have a clean mind (2 Cor. 10:4–5; 11:3). Jesus said, "But I say to you that whoever looks at a woman to lust for her has already committed adultery with her in his heart" (Matt. 5:28). For that reason, believers shouldn't allow filthy thoughts to pollute their mind. This doesn't mean, though, that they won't be tempted with impure imaginations. A great evangelist once explained, "You can't be responsible if birds fly over your head, but it is your fault if they lodge in your hair."

But sinful thoughts involve more than sex. A whole variety of lusts is involved. Some lust for money, while others lust for things that consume the mind. The Tenth Commandment commands, "You shall not covet your neighbor's house . . . wife . . . nor anything that is your neighbor's" (Ex. 20:17).

Sinful thoughts lead to sinful actions. As a man "thinks in his heart, so is he" (Prov. 23:7). Before Eve sinned by eating the forbidden fruit, she lusted in her mind. Paul warned, "But I fear, lest somehow, as the serpent deceived Eve by his craftiness, so your minds may be corrupted from the simplicity that is in Christ" (2 Cor. 11:3). The first step toward sin begins with your mind thinking about the act. So as Christians you must discipline your thoughts. The Bible describes this as "bringing every thought into captivity to the obedience of Christ" (2 Cor. 10:5).

5. *Christians must discipline themselves to keep their body spiritually clean.* Some have the attitude, "My soul lives forever, so I'll ignore the body." As a result, a person may overfeed (gluttony) his already fat body, open himself to lung cancer by smoking, or indulge in alcohol leading to possible addiction or even cirrhosis of the liver. Christians cannot separate their body from their Christian duty. Paul asks, "Surely you know that you are God's temple and that God's Spirit lives in you!" (1 Cor. 3:16, TEV). The way Christians treat their body reflects their discipline toward spiritual things and vice versa.

The little child stamps his feet, "I can do what I want." Yet the parent knows if the child plays in an open fire, he could receive a permanent scar. The teen may enjoy smoking pot because it feels good, but some people are saying that later in life that teen may experience blackouts when faced with any pressure or tension. Rather than becoming a dedicated disciple of Jesus Christ, the teen develops an emotional crutch when facing problems.

6. *Christians must discipline their relationship to others so that the decisions of others will not cause them to stumble.* Christians' friends are important for they help to determine their outlook on life. But the Bible does warn, "Do not be unequally yoked together with unbelievers" (2 Cor. 6:14). This does not mean that Christians shouldn't work at the same store with non-Christians or join the same club. It does mean they should not link themselves with an unsaved person in marriage or in any other way wherein a decision by unbeliever will determine the direction of their Christian life.

The Bible teaches, " 'Come out from among them and be separate, says the Lord. Do not touch what is unclean, and I will receive you.' 'I will be a Father to you, and you shall be My sons and daughters' " (2 Cor. 6:17–18). This verse teaches that Christians should not get involved with people whose decisions will destroy their walk with Christ.

7. *Christians must discipline themselves so they don't adversely influence others.* When Cain killed Abel, he asked, "Am I my brother's keeper?" Many have repeated that question, implying they are not responsible for others. However, John Donne observed, "No man is an island." Christians live in a human community where every action is influenced by and has an impact on others.

The Bible uses the phrase *stumbling block* to teach that it's wrong to harm others by negative influence. Paul warns, "But beware lest somehow this liberty of yours become a stumbling block to those who are weak" (1 Cor. 8:9). That means that Christians can't do everything they want to do, especially if their actions would bring harm to others. This is a spiritual perspective. A Christian's liberty must not hurt others spiritually.

In many Mediterranean villages, meat that had first been sacrificed to idols was sold in butcher shops. New Christians who had previously worshiped idols refused to eat meat offered to idols because they felt they were compromising by recognizing idols, that is, sinning against their conscience. However, a few Christians did eat meat offered to idols, saying "hamburger was hamburger." Paul believed this opinion, "For neither if we eat are we the better, nor if we do not eat are we the worse" (1 Cor. 8:8). However, Paul says it was wrong if he hurt other people by what he ate. "If food makes my brother stumble, I will never again eat meat, lest I make my brother stumble" (1 Cor. 8:13). What is the principle for today? Christians must discipline themselves, making sure they don't harm other Christians by their "liberty."

All Christians are tempted to sin. Because of this, Christians must discipline themselves to always say "no" to temptation. Paul notes that Christians must remember that "the temptations in your life are no different from what others experience. And God is faithful. He will not allow the temptation to be more than you can stand. When you are tempted, he will show you a way out so that you can endure" (1 Cor. 10:13, NLT). The issue is not whether Christians are tempted, but how they will respond. Christians can and must discipline themselves to say "no." However, to be victorious over temptation, believers should constantly practice avoiding areas of temptation.

When Christians yield to temptation, and undoubtedly, they will, they shouldn't let one sin destroy their walk with God. Apply God's prescription for restoring fellowship with

Him: "If we confess our sins, He is faithful and just to forgive us our sins and to cleanse us from all unrighteousness" (1 John 1:9). Confession means to agree with God about sin. Christians agree that sin is terrible, and it will destroy their Christian testimony. "He who covers his sins will not prosper" (Prov. 28:13). But notice the next part of that verse: "But whoever confesses and forsakes them will have mercy."

Learn to Live a Righteous Life

A teenage girl stood on the ledge of a burning building. The fireman on the hook and ladder couldn't get any closer to her than a handclasp.

"Grab my arm, and I'll grab yours. Just jump. Trust me," he shouted.

In a similar manner, learning constant victory over sin has the same two ingredients. One must leave sin and jump into God's arms. To have deliverance, there must be a leap of faith. However, the Divine Fireman is not limited by human ability. A believer's deliverance is in Jesus Christ.

One can't keep rocking in a chair and then pray to God to take away the dizziness he gets from rocking. He must leave the source of temptation. God expects believers to live separated from sin and separated unto righteousness. It is not enough that one quits sinning; he must live a holy life. Sometimes this is called the victorious Christian life. The Christian must learn and practice the following "disciplines" to experience victory.

1. Christians learn "discipline" by allowing their new nature to control their life. Paul said, "Therefore, when anyone receives Christ, he becomes a new creation; things from his old life have passed away; behold, he has new desires to serve God" (2 Cor. 5:17, author translation). Sap that runs in a dormant tree in the spring can illustrate these new desires. The sap (new life) pushes off the dead leaves, as the believers' new desires that come from their new nature begin pushing the old habits out of their life.

A program of discipline or reform is not enough. Counting to ten when you get angry is not God's way of victory. God has given you a new nature that can control your anger, but you must allow this new nature to control your life. This is a discipline that must be learned.

Distaste for the things of the world will grow as you acquire a taste for spiritual things. Some habits will drop off immediately, while other habits will take longer.

2. Christians learn the discipline of expressing gratitude to God for what Christ has done for them. Paul wrote, "And whatever you do in word or deed, do all in the name of the Lord Jesus, giving thanks to God the Father through Him" (Col. 3:17).

Believers dishonor Christ when they continue to be controlled by their old sinful habits. The Bible describes those in an unsaved state as "sons of disobedience" (Eph. 2:2). Once people become Christians, they want to obey God. All they do should glorify God. If Christians cannot thank Christ for something they do, they had better avoid it.

3. Christians must discipline themselves to watch for the dangers and miseries that sin breeds. I heard of a professor who was rushed to the hospital with stomach cramps. Tests revealed nothing. A month later the entire family went to the emergency room with the same symptoms. Again, they could find nothing. A friend with whom they had gone to Mexico called them about a potential cause. They had both bought Mexican pottery that was not properly kiln dried.

The lead paint was melting into their hot chocolate, causing sickness.

Although improperly fired pottery is not a sin, the same principle applies. A Christian's sin may affect his whole family. A believer may not be offended by some of the "new" movies, but his teenage children could be eaten up with passion.

You can't get every evil influence out of your life, because you do live in an evil world, but you can develop a discipline to watch for those things that would harm you. Jesus prayed, "I do not pray that You should take them out of the world, but that You should keep them from the evil one" (John 17:15).

4. Christians must discipline themselves to maintain a strong testimony for Christ. After I was saved, I worried about being a poor testimony to some of my friends. *How can I keep myself clean?* I thought. I told one high school buddy I was sorry for the things we had done together before my salvation. He never came around me again.

The Bible demands that a Christian "abstain from every form of evil" (1 Thess. 5:22). Paul said,

When I wrote to you before, I told you not to associate with people who indulge in sexual sin. But I wasn't talking about unbelievers who indulge in sexual sin, or who are greedy, or cheat people, or idol worshipers. You would have to leave this world to avoid people like that. I meant was that you are not to associate with anyone who claims to be a believer yet indulges in sexual sin, or is greedy, or worships idols, or is abusive, or a drunkard, or cheats people. Don't even eat with such people. (1 Cor. 5:9–11, NLT)

You have to maintain contact with unsaved people in order to be a witness to them, but not necessarily with "sinning" Christians. As a Christian, you must protect your testimony.

5. *Christians must discipline themselves to live by priorities.* If you only have limited time for reading, you probably should not spend it all on casual reading or on entertaining items. Jesus said, "Seek first the kingdom of God" (Matt. 6:33). The first priority in the life of a believer is spiritual maturity. You should read Christian books and magazines that will enrich your life. You should spend time with your Bible, but this doesn't mean you shouldn't read the newspapers or entertaining items. Matthew 6:33 continues, ". . . and all these things shall be added to you." The principle is that you should give priority of time, money, and energy to achieve spiritual growth, and other activities take second or third place.

6. *Christians should discipline themselves because they are preparing themselves for heaven.* There will be no evil in heaven, so living apart from evil here on earth gives a foretaste of heaven.

The young girl stops dating other men the minute she falls in love with her future husband. She doesn't wait until the wedding ceremony to stop going out with other men. She prepares herself to live with one man by spending time with him. In the same way, Christians should get ready to spend all eternity with the bridegroom, Jesus Christ. Those who don't like the thought of living for Him only may have something wrong with their walk with God.

Christians should separate from the evils of this life, and live as though they were already in heaven. Paul said, "We, however, are citizens of heaven, and we eagerly wait for our Savior, the Lord Jesus Christ, to come from heaven" (Phil. 3:20, TEV). Until that day comes, however, you must determine to live a pure life. Paul said, "Now may the God of peace Himself sanctify you completely; and may your whole spirit, soul, and body be preserved blameless at the coming of our Lord Jesus Christ" (1 Thess. 5:23).

An acquaintance of mine was having a problem with his car—it was sputtering and losing its power. His mechanic checked out the spark plugs, fuel pump, distributor, and still couldn't find the problem. Finally, the mechanic's boss told him to blow out the fuel line. A little bit of trash was causing the problem. There was not enough grit to fill a quarter of a teaspoon, yet it was enough to make the car lose its power. Sin is like trash in the fuel line, making the Christian lose his ability to do the will of God and fall into bad habits.

Make Victory the Goal of Living

While preaching to a small congregation in Northern Ontario, I saw a great moving of the Spirit; twenty-seven people came forward for salvation in a church of eighty-five people. I knelt with a man at the church altar. "I've got a hideous sin in my life," the church leader confessed to me. All sin is hideous in God's sight, but by human judgments, I didn't think his sin was all that terrible.

"I must have victory," so he poured out his soul to God in prayer. His sincerity and agony moved me. Never had I seen a man who wanted victory over a habit more than this church leader.

This is the heart of the true child of God. He wants to please God and be pure from sin. He is willing to discipline every area of life to gain a spiritual relationship with God. I wish every Christian wanted victory over sin as this man did. Perhaps some don't want it because they don't know what victory is and what it can do for them.

Think about It

Question: What is the main motivation for a Christian to discipline his life?

Answer: Some Christians develop spiritual habits and discipline their life because of their deep love for God. There is a positive reason for self-control and self-discipline.

Other Christians have been hurt from sin. They have touched the fire and they know what a searing burn feels like. They don't want to get burned again, so they discipline themselves to stay away from fire.

God uses a number of different reasons to help His people learn self-discipline. But you should never discipline your life because of legalism. That's when you keep a rule for the sake of keeping it. Legalism is simply "behavior modification." You should always look beyond the rule or principle, and do what is right for an eternal purpose. You need to discipline yourself because of your relationship with Christ and for the glory of God.

8

❖

CHRISTIANITY IS A UNIQUE WORLDVIEW

Four blind men were introduced to an elephant and asked to describe the animal they could not see. The first man reached out and touched the elephant's trunk and concluded that an elephant is like a large hose. The second man touched the elephant's leg and concluded that an elephant is like the trunk of a tree. The third man touched the elephant's large body and concluded that an elephant is like a wall. The fourth man touched the elephant's tail and concluded that an elephant is like a rope. The four blind men touched the same elephant, but came up with four different views of the elephant. Each defined the elephant based on his personal experience, and each accurately described what they experienced. But they were all wrong! Their failure to see the whole elephant resulted in their defective description.

Today, people have many different, often conflicting, ways to describe life and the world. Some see the human race as essentially good while others view people as basically evil. Some see the world as coming to be through the process known as evolution. Christians see the world as the handiwork of the Creator. Some say man is the center of this universe, while Christians see everything in life centering around a sovereign God and everything in life heading toward His conclusion. In each case, everyone has values that are foundational to the way they view the world and their function in this life.

Christianity's outlook on life is a unique worldview consisting of a series of non-negotiable values that form the uniquely Christian view of life. The Christian worldview is theocentric (viewing God at the center of all life), not man-centered (the humanistic worldview that says man is the center of everything). The Christian worldview is the result of examining all the evidence to see the big picture of God's plan for the world (God controls all the trillions of stars) and the microscopic view of God's plan for each individual (God's power holds each atom together, Col. 1:17).

Many Ways to Define Our World

We live in an age of options, so it's not surprising that different people view life in many different ways. Choices are a core value in a multicultural and pluralistic society. So, in the world's new global village, diversity is celebrated. When our parents or grandparents ate in a restaurant, it was probably a family restaurant in the community that featured a daily special. Even though there were other choices available, most customers ordered the special. But today is different! Today's families live by choices. One night they eat Mexican, the next night Italian, and the following night Chinese.

While our bodies adjust to the various foods we ingest, our minds face a similar challenge. We live in a world colored by a variety of different and incompatible worldviews. One person believes he has evolved from a piece of slime on the back side of a rock in the primeval ocean. The evolutionist treats the human race as an animal that must adjust its behavior to its environment. The existentialist points humanity toward self-perception and self-discovery so he can master his own destiny. The capitalist advocates personal financial prosperity for a prosperous materialistic lifestyle. The Marxist insists that capitalistic greed keeps the masses poor, so the Communist lives for the common good of the party. The Eastern mystic advocates passive resistance. The fundamentalist Muslim recruits terrorist suicide bombers to destroy the great Satan—the capitalistic foreigners.

In previous generations, American values were largely passed on through the extended family, schools, churches, and associations that were part of community life. These institutions spoke with a common voice; there was little variance from its norm.

An individual was born into a culture that looked at life in a certain way and that became the way of interpreting the world. A generation later, a new generation was born and passed through the same "enculturation." Each generation usually developed the same worldview. But that's not true today. There are many voices telling people how to live and what values to hold. America doesn't have a perceived "right way" to understand the world.

In an age of tolerance, marked by an eagerness to find harmony among divergent worldviews, many argue it doesn't matter what you think; only actions matter. Of course, the way a person thinks always influences the way he acts.

I have a friend who was born in a Catholic hospital at the hands of a Jewish doctor into a conservative evangelical home. When asked what his religion is, he answers, "Confused."

The generation that has emerged out of the twentieth century has been inundated with many different messages, from many different voices, and the end result is a confused generation. Some are so confused they don't even recognize the confusion that dominates their thinking. They have difficulty evaluating different worldviews and cannot choose one that works for them. In their confusion, many have turned to what is called "the cafeteria option." Just as those who eat at a cafeteria choose from the many different food items, today people choose from various ways of looking at life to form their own blended worldview.

But there is danger in a worldview cafeteria. People who have choices at a cafeteria don't always eat nutritionally balanced meals. And those who seek to build a blended worldview from the many competing opinions often end up hurting themselves.

Dysfunctionalism is built into the cafeteria options because different worldviews are not totally compatible; they are often hostile to an individual's emotional and physical health. For instance, both Christianity and Islam believe in "one God," so many might think they would have much in common, but in reality they are radically opposed to one another. God is the center of each religion, but is defined differently by each faith community. No Muslim leader would ever claim Allah was "the God and Father of our Lord Jesus Christ." They would violently oppose that view, while that's a common description of God in the Christian Scriptures.

Questions for Your Worldview

A worldview is only helpful when it helps a person to accurately understand the world. In building a personal worldview, an individual must find the answers to the fundamental questions of life:

Where did I come from?

Why am I here?

Why do I suffer?

Where am I heading?

How do I know anything?

When a person can adequately answer these questions, he is beginning to understand his world. When Christian answers are compared with other worldviews, it becomes clear Christianity is a unique worldview.

Where Did I Come From?

The first imperative question is, "Where did I come from?"

A little boy ran into the kitchen to ask his mother where he came from. The mother thought it was too early to tell her young son about the birds and bees, but she launched into a long, involved explanation of conception. The boy interrupted to say, "I don't care about that! The boy down the street came from Toledo, and I just wanted to know where I came from."

We laugh at the misunderstanding about origins, but it's not a question of personal origins; it's a question of the origin of the human race. Where did the human race come from?

When we understand the origins of humankind, we have a context in which to understand life. This is why therapists often invest time studying the family history of their clients. But the question of origins is bigger than simply looking at one's family history. Charles Darwin said the original man came as a result of evolution—*The Origin of the Species*. The Christian disagrees, because the Bible teaches God created the first man in His image, therefore all people are accountable to their Creator.

Darwin's theory of evolution, that more complex beings evolved over time from less complex beings, is widely held in the popular culture as an adequate answer to this first question. Increasingly, in both the academic and scientific communities, Darwin's hypothesis is being questioned and challenged, but popular opinion is slow to change. Why? Because the American public schools almost universally assume evolution to be true and most Americans go along with evolution. If they believed God created man, they would be obligated to live by the "laws" of that Creator. Because most want to be free of external restraints, they reject creation and opt for evolution.

There are four questions Darwinian evolutionists have not been able to answer. The first is, "Where is the missing link?" When evolutionary paleontologists arrange and measure the brain capacity between the primate and a human being, there is a significant gap between the human and the next closest primate, with no credible fossil record to prove otherwise. Darwin's theory has no objective facts to link animals to the human race.

The second question relates to the process of change by which evolution happens. When mutations are observed within species, they tend to be degenerative and result in an inferior derivation. It is therefore reasonable to ask how can man evolve to be the apex (the highest) of living beings if all the facts suggest the process of evolution goes the opposite way, that is, it devolves?

The third difficult question for the evolutionist relates to the origin of life itself. Christians teach creation came *ex nihilo*—that God created everything from nothing. Further, both evolutionary scientists and Christian creationists would agree that spontaneous generation does not presently exist in today's universe. Therefore, the evolutionist cannot answer the question where life originated. Evolutionists have no explanation for the source of life, if there is not a God to supply it.

Finally, there is adamant and often unreasonable opposition by evolutionists to intelligent design. The normal response by the scientific community is to study and gather data to determine the validity of any and all theories. But evolutionists refuse to even examine the claims of Scripture. They presuppose the laws of evolution, but refuse to admit there is a lawgiver. They see a well-balanced operating universe but refuse to believe or even explore data that suggests *intelligent design*.

Christians believe God (His intelligent design) created everything out of nothing. The Bible begins with the statement, "In the beginning God created the heavens and the earth" (Gen. 1:1). The apostle John affirms, "All things were made through Him, and without Him nothing was made that was made" (John 1:3). The writer of Hebrews stated "that the worlds were framed by the word of God, so that the things which are seen were not made of things which are visible" (Heb. 11:3). Creation by God is foundational to the very nature of the Christian faith.

One of many examples of the harmony of science and the Scriptures is found in the basic laws of nature. Our physical world is governed by laws of nature that are consistent and unchanging. The existence of these laws suggests there is a lawgiver who was behind the origin of the universe. Christians believe that God created everything and established laws by which the world is governed.

The inherent unity of the human race is yet another phenomenon best explained by a Christian worldview. Paul told the Athenians, "He has made from one blood every nation of men to dwell on the face of the earth, and has determined their preappointed times and the boundaries of their dwellings" (Acts 17:26). That presupposition is the basis upon which various people groups relate to one another and work together to achieve some measure of harmony between nations and ethnic communities. In contrast, if humanity came into being through various "mutant humans" in different parts of the world, there is no essential reason for unity within the human race and no ethical reason to insist that respect be shown to various people groups.

Christians believe that God created the human race and therefore, individuals cannot live independent of God. Believers view people as the highest expression of God's creation on earth and responsible for the proper management of the planet. While Christians understand that people are limited in many ways, they also affirm that a human being is something wonderful. They believe the ability of people to think, feel, and choose is a reflection of the very image of God in which they were created.

Why Am I Here?

If I am in fact a created being, then I have been created for a reason. However, if I am simply the result of random chance, it is difficult to believe I have a significant purpose in life. As culture increasingly rejects its Christian foundation, it struggles to find a higher reason worth living for.

Materialism is one dominant worldview that suggests wealth and prosperity are the most valid reasons for living. This view is best expressed by the bumper sticker that defines the golden rule as "He who has the most gold rules." But one should learn from the stories of the affluent that they have difficulty finding personal fulfillment and meaning in wealth accumulation.

There appears to be a new materialism emerging that seeks to address this problem of selfishness and greed by using wealth for the welfare of others, that is, the relief of poverty, the advancement of education, etc. While this altered way of thinking may bring a sense of purpose and meaning to some, still the question remains, "Is helping others in and of itself a big enough reason to explain why I'm here?"

While Christians believe humanitarian efforts are good, even essential, there must be a higher reason for helping others. Christians believe they exist to glorify God and serve God. One way of serving God is helping others.

The old Presbyterian catechism began with the question, "What is the chief end of man?" The answer was, "to glorify God and enjoy Him forever." This question pointed a person to God and His purpose for an individual's life. Jesus taught, "God is Spirit, and those who worship Him must worship in spirit and truth" (John 4:23). That means the purpose of life is to worship God and serve Him.

The essential difference between materialism and Christianity is the difference between man and God. Materialism is an anthropocentric worldview, expressed in the attitude, "What's in it for me?" On the other hand, Christians have a theocentric worldview. Paul summarized this worldview, "For to me, to live is Christ, and to die is gain" (Phil. 2:21).

Why Do I Suffer?

Problems and pain are part of the human experience and often lead to the question, "Why do I suffer?" This question must be answered by every worldview trying to interpret life. Once again, the answer to this question marks the Christian worldview as unique from others.

One of the core values of Islam is submission to God, a value also held by Christians. But in contrast with Christians, Muslims have difficulty finding any force that influences life outside of God. Therefore, when it comes to the question, "Why do I suffer?" the response of Islam is simply, "It is the will of Allah."

The problem of suffering is a difficult question for Christians, who also believe life works best when a person submits to God and His will. But Christians know that God does not cause suffering because He is good, and He loves His people. A good God could not hurt people. Christians believe suffering comes from conditions in this world, not from God.

The human race was created perfect with certain liberties including the freedom to fail. The biblical account of the creation of humanity includes a specific warning from God: "But of the tree of the knowledge of good and evil you shall not eat, for in the day that you eat of it you shall surely die" (Gen. 2:17). The Hebrew word translated "surely die" describes death as both a process and event, that is, "dying you will die" (author's translation). Because the first couple failed to keep God's command, suffering and the process of "dying" were introduced into the human race.

Death, disease, and suffering are the result of the Fall. The first couple, Adam and Eve, eventually died. Disease produces toxins in the body, which eventually lead to death. These toxins often are the physical cause of severe pain.

In this sense, suffering is the result of the human race's failure to obey God and live in harmony with Him in the garden. Christians believe God uses conviction, failure, and pain as centripetal forces to draw people back to Himself. Ultimately, the Christian worldview includes the promise that full restoration with God ultimately leads to a pain-free existence in the next life.

Where Am I Heading?

Hope is essential to life. Therefore, an adequate worldview must address the issue of hope and answer the question, "Where am I heading?"

The existentialist believes that each person is the master of his own destiny and leaves the answer to that question to the individual. Many eastern religions teach the idea of "the circle of life." Western media has popularized this concept when it claims that life is cyclical—an individual is born, he lives, he dies, and he is reborn to repeat the process. While that view may provide some measure of superficial comfort for those facing death, is life really that meaningless?

Christians answer that question differently, suggesting different destinations for different people. They believe that the Christian, at death, enters the presence of God. Paul wrote, "We are confident . . . to be absent from the body and to be present with the Lord" (2 Cor. 5:8). Christians also believe God has prepared a place for them to spend eternity. John witnessed, "Now I saw a new heaven and a new earth, for the first heaven and the first earth had passed away" (Rev. 21:1). What makes heaven so attractive is the presence of God Himself. "Behold the tabernacle of God is with men, and He will dwell with them, and they shall be His people" (Rev. 21:3).

But within a Christian worldview, not everyone goes to heaven. "It is appointed for men to die once, but after this the judgment" (Heb. 9:27). At this judgment, the secrets of the hearts of each person will be revealed (Rom. 2:16). Then all who have rejected God will be faced with the consequence of their sin (Rom. 6:23). Those who have rejected God's gracious offer of eternal life will be left with only one other alternative, a place of eternal retribution described as "the lake of fire" (Rev. 20:15) and "the second death" (Rev. 21:8). Christians further believe God is "not willing that any should perish but that all should come to repentance" (2 Pet. 3:9). For that reason, the hope of eternal life is held out to all until they finally reject God.

While the Christian view differs from the existentialist view that an individual is the master of his own destiny, they do agree each person is responsible for his own destiny. The driver is the one who controls the bus; he sits in the driver's seat during the trip. Christians do not believe they are in the driver's seat. They know that God is in the driver's seat, but they believe that each person must choose to get on God's bus at the terminal.

How Do I Know Anything?

The final big question to be addressed in a worldview is, "How do I know anything?" This is one of the essential philosophical questions of life. Once again, the Christian's answer to this question separates him from alternative ways of thinking about living life in general.

Christianity is an objective faith based on authoritative revelation. One core value of the Christian worldview is best expressed in the words of a children's chorus, "Jesus loves me, this I know, for the Bible tells me so." Why do Christians know that Jesus loves them? Not because they're good and not because they're obedient, but because the Bible tells them so. The Christian believes the Bible is the authoritative revelation from God.

In this respect, Christianity is unique from other religious worldviews. Christians have confidence in their relationship to God (2 Tim. 1:12). Most other religious people don't have this confidence and their objective minds tend to be clouded by their subjective experiences.

Christians believe they can think, know things, arrive at rational conclusions, and remember. Christians believe God expects them to use their minds in every aspect of life. They are rational because they are made in the image of God—who is rational. God never asks a person to deposit his brain at the church door and "just believe." God says, "Come now let us reason together" (Isa. 1:18). Christianity is a rational religion and all of humankind's criteria for truth and rationality fit perfectly with Christianity.

Think about It

Question: How can we know that Christianity actually explains life as we know it?

Answer: Christianity is true. Truth is defined as that which is consistent within itself and that which corresponds (fits within) life as it exists. First, Christianity is a consistent belief system. It answers all the questions of life and the answers perfectly correspond to one another. Second, Christianity is a belief system that provides satisfying life systems for all who follow Jesus Christ, whether they are men or women, rich or poor, young or old, and it perfectly works in all cultures of the world.

This belief system has produced some of the greatest expressions of civilization known to humankind and has given the greatest quality of life, to the greatest number of persons, for the complete scope of their individual lives and their corporate civilization.

9

CHRISTIANITY IS AN INTERACTIVE COMMUNITY

Jesus answered clearly and without hesitation when asked to identify the greatest commandment, " 'You shall love the LORD your God with all your heart, and with all your soul, and with all your mind.' This is the first and great commandment. And the second is like it: 'You shall love your neighbor as yourself' " (Matt. 22:37–39). And since an individual can't have a relationship with just himself, relationships are at the heart of what it means to be a Christian. Salvation begins as a relationship with God, and it should be expressed in one's relationships with others. And to make this happen, Jesus established a new institution—the church. But many people don't treat the church as a church.

The Barna Poll suggests most people today want to know God, but wish to do so outside the established church. There are many reasons why people have such a negative view of the church today. The public loses confidence over public scandals involving high-profile Christian leaders, the sexual escapades of evangelical pastors, and the news reports of Roman Catholic priests sexually molesting young boys.

The media continues to emphasize declining church attendance. And many who have checked out the church have insurmountable problems with the church. They are turned off by long-standing church traditions that have little personal meaning for them. Some have been turned off because the church preaches against the way people dress, or presents a list of rules as the basis for living the Christian life. They see the church advocating an expected lifestyle that seems out of date and foreign to today's contemporary culture. Others see the church as "ingrown" and this unwittingly communicates the message, "You will never really belong here."

Finally, the public is turned off when churches fight over whether to sing traditional hymns with organ accompaniment or contemporary songs with lifted hands and a praise band accompaniment. The louder the band, the louder some criticize.

Despite the criticism, most Christians realize the church's real nature is "the church, which is his body" (Eph. 1:22–23, KJV). All believers are members of Christ's body, where each person has a place and function (1 Cor. 12). Therefore, all believers are responsible to care for one another.

In earlier chapters, it was shown Jesus indwelt believers (Gal. 2:20). Now it must be emphasized that Jesus indwells the church, "For where two or three are gathered together in My name, I am there in the midst of them" (Matt. 18:20). There it is—the church is a body of people.

Didn't Jesus did promise, "I will build My church" (Matt. 16:18)? Despite the shortcomings of the early church,

John described seeing seven churches as candlesticks and Jesus walking "in the middle of the churches" (Rev. 1:12–13, author translation). Perhaps if the church were the church that Jesus wants it to be, people would be attracted to His light as He shines like candlesticks.

What Does a Church Look Like?

In the New Testament the word *church* is applied to small intimate house-churches, to the huge gatherings on Solomon's Porch in the Temple, and to all true believers in the universal church (1 Thess. 1:1; Acts 2:47, 3:11; Eph. 1:22–23). What does the church look like today?

When many people think of the church, they think of a building with a steeple or particular congregation they attended as a youth. The old Gaelic term *kirk* from which the English word "church" is derived was often used to describe "the Kirk of Scotland" (the Presbyterian Church) or a local church in the community—the kirk. At other times also, the term *church* describes a building on the corner, or a denomination. But the Bible never refers to the church as a building or denomination. *Church* was a term describing a real community of believers who meet in the presence of Christ. A church is not described by what Christians do, but who they are. But over time a problem arose. Christians began going to church, rather than being the church. Then outsiders began seeing church as a place rather than a way of life.

From the beginning, the church was a gathering of Christians, committed to a common purpose (the Great Commission), and they shared the core value of loving God (the Great Commandment).

Individuals who join an institutional church, do so because they want the close fellowship and/or interrelationship with other believers. But the average church in America has eighty-seven people in attendance each week, a little bit too big to enjoy intimacy. So they sit in pews looking at the backs of people's heads and listening to a minister preach to them.

Is this what a church is all about?

A church community is a bonding of people. True believers are looking for a sense of family or oneness with other people; they want to feel a part of a "faith-based community." The very nature of a church community is the shared experience of many people. Christians share their dreams, problems, and resources, and then others reciprocate. At that point the church becomes a sharing community.

Probably, the smaller the church, the easier it is for all to experience community. As a church expands, taking in more individuals—with different viewpoints—it becomes more difficult to experience community. Today's infatuation with the megachurch makes community difficult.

One common thread, though, is that each person in the church community has the same profound experience to share. They have met Jesus Christ in a born-again experience; they understand, both verbally and nonverbally, what is involved in that experience. Because they understand each other's secrets (the experiences they can't verbalize), they are able to interact with one another at a nonverbal or experiential level.

A community allows for diversity. When people become a part of community, they usually affirm their faith in an interactive identity with the faith-statement of the church community. They know one another, know what other people believe, and they recognize the values and attitudes of other people. But most importantly, they know the life-changing experience that others have experienced. Therefore, they trust others in the church community, perhaps more than they would trust anyone else in other groups.

But that doesn't mean every person in a church community absolutely agrees with every other person in all aspects of life. They all agree on the importance of the born-again experience, the effects of regeneration, and the principles under which they live. Everyone in a church community shares these values and attitudes; however, there probably are many other experiences in secular life where the members may disagree.

People will differ when it comes to recreation, relaxation, reading habits, or television shows. While community brings a certain oneness among believers, it also allows for diversity among its members. Actually, diversity is the glue that holds individuals in the church community and allows everyone to remain unique and different.

Community does not stress conformity in every area of life. People in a church community do not dress the same, do not eat the same food, do not drive the same kind of cars, nor do they work at the same type of employment. The glue that gives them cohesiveness to their church community also allows them to be different outside the church meeting.

But community does encourage hospitality. Members of a church should serve one another, respect one another, and in a true sense of the Scriptures, love one another. This means they accept one another as a unique individual within the community. As a result, there is freedom in community, while at the same time there is oneness in the community.

Because a church community is held together by shared experiences, the bond that holds individuals to the community is never indoctrination to a doctrinal statement. Some churches do have written creeds. To become a part of that community, a person must ascribe to a specific doctrinal statement. But the church community that Jesus established, His body, is far deeper than a doctrinal agreement. Why is it? The glue that bonds them as a community is their transformation by Christ—Christ indwells each one, and they share this common experience with one another.

A community helps nurture faith. Christians often think faith is nurtured in a classroom where the teacher passes out a doctrinal statement and then explains the meaning of each doctrine to the students. The students may learn it and commit it to memory, however, this is not the same as making the statements of Christianity a part of one's life. It is simply indoctrination.

However, when faith is nurtured within a community, faith is an action. It's something that a person does, that is, faith is the total person's response to God. On the other hand, when faith is a noun, it is usually a doctrinal statement, that is, the sum total of what a person believes. Both living faith and doctrinal faith are important and necessary, but which one comes first? Obviously, living faith, nurtured in a community, comes first.

A person's faith is formed, generally, as he reads the Scriptures. "Faith comes by hearing, and hearing by the word of God" (Rom. 10:17). But a person also gains faith as he interacts with God. This faith formation usually happens in a community where young believers see older believers following Jesus Christ. They see the older believers step out in faith, and they follow the same example. So their faith is both formed and nurtured in a community, i.e., with other people.

It's in a church community that young believers get a desire to serve God and begin to find places where they can serve. It may begin with small tasks in the community and then grow to greater areas of responsibility and accountability. Within this community, young believers discover their spiritual gifts and calling.

The new believers develop values and attitudes by which they will live in the church community. As these values and attitudes become important to them, they find they must be honest, pure, obedient to God, and serve other people. Their commitment to these values gives them an identity. In their commitment they discover who they are (followers of Jesus Christ), and discover how they are growing (in their loyalty to Jesus Christ).

A church community is a community of conviction. Most churches are not held together by written principles, standards of conduct, signed covenants, or pledges. Rather people are drawn to a community as they interact with the values and attitudes of other believers in the church. Everyone in a church community has a deep commitment to the values and experiences of one another. In this sense, churches become communities of conviction. They have a shared sense of how to live for God, and this is what makes a church so attractive.

A community is a mentoring agent. When new Christians enter a church, they are not taught what to believe, nor do they learn how to practice the Christian life in the classroom. These are assimilated through nonverbal experiences. New believers are accepted for who they are, but they soon feel the pressure to hold the attitudes of others in the church, to live the way others are living, and to prize the things that others value. As a result, it's usually not any one individual who leads them into acceptance in the church. It's the community itself that becomes a mentoring agent.

Because a church offers a network of belonging in which young Christians feel recognized for who they are, as well as who they are becoming in Christ, the church community becomes its most powerful focus. Thus in mentoring, the church community does two things. First, it's challenging new believers to enter into community experience. And second, it's always supporting its members, no matter where they are in the spiritual pilgrimage of faith.

Seven Pictures of the Church

What we have seen is that the church is not a building or an organization, but an organism of living, growing believers. There are seven pictures, or metaphors, in the New Testament that describe a church. These pictures help in understanding the life and ministry of the church.

In the first picture, the apostle Paul describes the church as a *body*. Most often, he uses this metaphor to emphasize the need for every member in a body to be involved with every other member, using their unique gifts to complete the work of Christ. "For as the body is one and has many members, but all the members of that one body, being many, are one body, so also is Christ" (1 Cor. 12:12). In the event he had not been clear in stating this principle, Paul later adds, "Now you are the body of Christ, and members individually" (1 Cor. 12:27). Just as the body needs individual members (i.e., hands, feet, eyes, nose, etc.) to do their part to function well, so the church depends on each member doing his or her part to be the church God intends it to be.

The second picture is of a *building*. However, this reference does not mean Christians are to construct buildings. It's an analogy that refers to the foundation upon which a church community rests. Jesus told Peter he would build the church on Him, not Peter personally, but on his statement of faith—Peter's identification of Jesus as "the Christ, the Son of the Living God" (Matt. 16:16). "You are no longer strangers and foreigners, but fellow citizens with the saints and members of the household of God, having been built on the foundation of the apostles and prophets, Jesus Christ Himself being the chief cornerstone" (Eph. 2:19–20).

It's not surprising that Peter chose to describe the church in the context of a building on a foundation. Writing to Jewish Christians, Peter told them, "You also, as living stones, are being built up as a spiritual house" (1 Peter 2:5). This metaphor drawn from construction also emphasizes relationships. Only as all the stones in the structure are rightly related to each other is this "spiritual temple" built as a unique dwelling place of God.

The third picture of a church community is a *marriage*. When Paul talked about a Christian's love relationship to God, he described it as a relationship between Christ and His church. Evangelism is betrothing "a chaste virgin to Christ," whom Paul describes as the husband (2 Cor. 11:2). In the custom of first-century Jewish marriages, this was the first phase of the marriage process.

Later, Paul described the relationship between husbands and wives in the context of "a great mystery . . . concerning

Christ and the church" (Eph. 5:32). In that context, husbands were called upon to model Christ's love for the church in their relationship with their wives. "Husbands, love your wives, just as Christ also loved the church and gave Himself for her, that He might sanctify and cleanse her with the washing of water by the word, that He might present her to Himself a glorious church, not having spot or wrinkle or any such thing, but that she should be holy and without blemish" (Eph. 5:25–27). The response of the wife to her husband was to follow and respect his leadership (Eph. 5:24, 33). This is the ideal response of the bride/church toward her husband, the Lord Jesus Christ.

The fourth picture of a church was the relationship between Shepherd and sheep, that is, the church is a *sheepfold*. John the Baptist described Jesus as "the Lamb of God" (John 1:29), and Jesus described Himself, "I am the good shepherd. The good shepherd gives His life for the sheep" (John 10:11). Then Jesus described the church as a sheepfold (a pen where sheep are kept): "Other sheep I have which are not of this fold" (John 10:16). The church is a flock that follows the Shepherd. Jesus noted of His church, "Them also I must bring, and they will hear My voice; and there will be one flock" (John 10:16). There is much emphasis in Scripture about the relationship of the Shepherd and sheep, but perhaps this relationship is best summarized in Psalm 23, "Because the Lord is my Shepherd, I have everything I need" (Ps. 23:1, TLB).

The fifth picture that represents a church is a *garden*—the growth of plants, vines, or trees. Jesus uses the metaphor of a vine to describe His relationship to individual Christian believers: "I am the true vine, and My Father is the vinedresser" (John 15:1). This was Jesus' way of describing the unbreakable bond that existed between Himself and those who trust in Him. In the context of this metaphor, the vine is lifted up and pruned to insure it produces its greatest potential (John 15:2). The emphasis of the metaphor is an abiding relationship between Christ and believers, "I am the vine, you are the branches. He who abides in Me, and I in him, bears much fruit; for without Me you can do nothing" (John 15:5).

The sixth picture of the church is a *family*, where believers are called children or sons of God. The family is the foundational social institution of society. In this description, a family connects the father to his children. Jesus described the experience of becoming a Christian in the context of being "born again" (John 3:3, 7). In that context, "as many as received Him, to them He gave the right to become children of God, to those who believe in His name" (John 1:12). When teaching His disciples to pray, Jesus urged them to address God as their Father in heaven (Matt. 6:9; Luke 11:2). Christians throughout history have referred to one another as "brothers and sisters" because of this description of the church as the family of God.

The seventh picture of the church is a *priesthood*. While this analogy is foreign to the thinking of most in Western culture, the Jews who originally received the Scriptures quickly recognized it. Peter, whose primary ministry focused on introducing people from a Jewish background to Christianity, portrays the church as a priesthood working together in the service of God. He describes Christians as "a holy priesthood" (1 Peter 2:5) and "a royal priesthood" (1 Peter 2:9).

While some Christian denominations today use the word "priest" to designate a specific clergy office, the early church viewed every believer as a priest with direct access to God. Jesus Himself held the office of High Priest, and all other believers were viewed as "a kingdom of priests" (Rev. 1:6, literal translation). Most evangelical Christians describe this doctrine as "the priesthood of believers." It's significant that this metaphor is always used in the plural, suggesting a team approach to the priesthood—believers working together to accomplish their responsibilities before God. In the context of the Hebrew priesthood, the duties of the priests involved the worship of God, praying to God on behalf of others, and systematically teaching the word of God to others.

God designed the church to be a place where interactive relationships help believers to experience God. Christians gather together for corporate worship, the reading of the Scriptures, and a message to encourage and challenge them as they live life. While a growing number of people try to nourish their Christian life through various media ministries and Internet Web sites, that alone is not enough. People need face-to-face encounters with each other that will hold them accountable to their shared faith. While Christianity is often viewed as a private religious experience, it's also a corporate expression of faith and worship. What is Christianity all about? Christianity is seen in the church—the body of Christ. Without a church, many would not understand Christianity.

Think about It

Question: What is it about local churches that so many misunderstand Christianity? What can churches do to become a better reflection of Christianity?

Answer: People misunderstand Christianity because of the attitude of Christians toward their local church and the way local churches act. There are times when Christians fight in their churches about things of little or no consequence. At other times, the church fights the world or cultural practices around them. Outsiders don't understand the reasons Christians fight. Their big concern is, "Why doesn't the church express more love to the world and to one another?"

It's probable that the church does need repentance. Some churches need to *repent* of the evil they cause and the confusion they sow into the world. Still other churches need *renewal*, which is when the believers recommit themselves to the biblical practices that Christ expects of them. Finally, churches need *revival*. This is defined as God pouring Himself out on His people (Joel 2:28). The answer to these concerns is God living among His people in the church. Then and only then will the world understand what Christianity is all about.

10

CHRISTIANITY IS A PRACTICAL RELIGION

When a person becomes a Christian, he has a new desire to serve Christ and do what are called "good works." As a matter of fact, if a person doesn't serve Christ by doing good deeds to others, that person is probably not truly saved. He is only professing Christianity.

In the broad sweep of history, Christianity can be measured by the number of hospitals it has established and the number of medical missionaries who have given free medicine and medical help. Christianity can be measured by the number of schools and colleges it has established to freely educate the masses. Christianity has donated food and clothing, and helped people build shelters—free of charge. It's almost impossible to number the acts of kindness that Christians have done in the name of Christ.

Good works are called the social gospel, the gospel of good works, or just social work. In many places Christianity ministers directly to the poor person who needs help (from the bottom up). In other places, Christians have labored to help the needy by improving housing and working conditions, and establishing hospitals, schools, etc. This is good works from the top down.

The First Great Awakening swept England in the 1700s under the preaching of John Wesley and George Whitefield. Most of those who came to know Christ were from the poor and ignorant working class. Wesley founded the Methodist Church based on his new "methods" to evangelize and disciple his converts. The Methodist Church stood in stark contrast to the Anglican Church, which was a state church, supported financially by the Crown, and every new English baby was baptized into the Anglican Church.

There was an Anglican church in every town, but it did little to help the indigents, the ignorant, and the needy. One Anglican church at Clapham Crossing, a rich district of London, became so involved in good works that other churches followed its example and became known as the Clapham sect. Its pastor, John Venn, was touched spiritually by the Wesleyan revival, and in turn, he touched the aristocrats in his church. William Wilberforce was disturbed over the slave trade, especially since its trafficking was done in British ships. Venn preached against slavery in the pulpit, Wilberforce preached against it in Parliament. Finally, after years of discouraging defeats, Wilberforce got the Foreign Slave Trade Bill of May, 1806, passed to ban slavery.

Granville Sharpe from the Clapham church worked to improve working conditions. Lord Ashley and Michael Sadler campaigned against child labor. Elizabeth Fry worked to improve the conditions of women. The Clapham Church is an example of the social gospel working to establish righteous laws and helping the helpless.

Another Christian organization known for helping others is the Salvation Army. Organized like the military army, its founder General William Booth was driven to reach the masses. He used the sound of a marching band, with the booming bass drum, to draw masses to street meetings. Here the gospel was preached. People were encouraged to repent, to come forward, and kneel to receive Christ.

General Booth discovered so many problems among the poor that it wasn't enough just to get them saved. His army organized soup lines to feed the hungry, orphanages to care for homeless children, hospitals for the poor, and homes for pregnant unmarried girls. As the Army grew larger because of its success in helping the poor, it branched out into every widening field of humanitarian aid.

When Booth was too old and feeble to attend the massive annual convention of the Army, the leaders asked that he write out his message to be read to the assembly. In response, General Booth sent a telegram with one word, "Others."

Even though Christians do good works, they believe they are saved by faith alone and apart from works. To support this view they quote Paul, "For by grace you have been saved through faith, and that not of yourselves; it is the gift of God, not of works, lest anyone should boast" (Eph. 2:8–9).

While it is true Christians are saved apart from good works, the Bible also teaches that faith without works is not genuine. Genuine faith always expresses itself in practical demonstrations of the love of God. An early church leader, James, who was also the brother of Jesus, wrote, "For as the body without the spirit is dead, so faith without works is dead also" (James 2:26). To his critics, he would respond,

"Show me your faith without your works, and I will show you my faith by my works" (James 2:18).

These statements seem contradictory and some say Paul and James disagreed. But that's not true. Paul, the great champion of justification by faith alone apart from works, also taught there must be a relationship between genuine faith and practical good works. Paul told a younger pastor, "This is a faithful saying, and these things I want you to affirm constantly, that those who have believed in God should be careful to maintain good works. These things are good and profitable to men" (Titus 3:8).

The Christian faith grew out of Judaic roots of the Old Testament. Constantly, Old Testament believers were exhorted to do good works. The prophet Micah was typical of this view when he wrote, "He has shown you, O man, what is good; and what does the LORD require of you but to do justly, to love mercy, and to walk humbly with your God?" (Micah 6:8).

The prophet Amos cried out, "Let justice run down like water, and righteousness like a mighty stream" (Amos 5:24). Jeremiah urged Judah's king, "Execute judgment and righteousness . . . do no wrong and do no violence to the stranger, the fatherless, or the widow, nor shed innocent blood in this place" (Jer. 22:3). Ezekiel appealed to the royal family in his day to "remove violence and plundering, execute justice and righteousness" (Ezek. 45:9). Hosea said God desired "mercy and not sacrifice, and the knowledge of God more than burnt offering" (Hos. 6:6).

The interchange of the words "justice" and "righteousness" in these and other statements illustrates the close relationship between the two concepts. Living a lifestyle marked by justice involves consistently being the right person (being righteous) while doing the right thing in the right way for the right reason at the right time.

The challenge for Christians to do good deeds is not easy to fulfill. Because believers often are motivated by selfish desires, most find the challenge to give time and energy to others beyond their capabilities. Because lust and greed are present in all people, it's difficult to give away money to the poor, and this becomes doubly difficult because most people who have accumulated wealth by hard work think the poor are lazy and deserve their economic punishment. That is why Jesus taught His disciples that the motivating force behind good works is love. The Old Testament prophet Micah called his listeners "to love mercy." Loving mercy begins with loving the God of mercy; then moves to loving those who need His mercy.

When asked to identify the greatest commandment in the Law, without hesitation Jesus responded, "You shall love the LORD your God with all your heart, with all your soul, and with all your mind" (Matt. 22:37). When Christians follow that commandment, it changes their priority in life. Then Jesus quickly added, "The second is like it: 'You shall love your neighbor as yourself' " (Matt. 22:39). When God's agenda becomes the Christian's agenda, it means he expresses his love in tangible ways such as giving medical care to the hurting, food to the hungry, and clothing to the naked. In politics, it means standing up for those who can't stand for themselves.

Throughout Scripture, God is described as a people-loving God (John 3:16). Unlike most people living in our world today, God shows no partiality in His dealings with people (Acts 10:34). In fact, God chooses to protect those who have no one else to help them (Prov. 22:22–23). He has a special concern for the disadvantaged and disenfranchised in society (Ps. 146:9). Abusing these people is of particular offense to God (Prov. 14:31).

When pressed to elaborate on His command to love one's neighbor, Jesus taught the parable of the Good Samaritan. One clear principle drawn from that parable is that loving one's neighbor involves crossing the normal social and ethnic barriers of life. The Good Samaritan went to bandage the wounds of a person from a different ethnic background. It involved taking the hurting man to an inn and paying for food and lodging. When asked "Who is my neighbor?" it's not just the person living next door; it's any needy person who requires help.

Christianity is all about helping other people. Typically, a church budget designates a large portion of its finances to meet the needs of the world. This item, usually called "benevolence," involves gifts from the corporate church to support hospitals, schools, orphanages, feeding programs, and a number of other humanitarian projects.

But there's also individual involvement. Christians donate their time, talent, and energies to visit the mission fields to help missionaries in practical projects. They give their time to prepare meals in a mission to feed the homeless so they can get a chance to preach the gospel to them. At other times, they do the same labor, not to gain an opportunity to preach, but they do good works just because they want to. They are doing what Jesus would do.

Think about It

Question: Since Christians don't have to do good works to get saved, what are the reasons why they do good works?

Answer: There are several reasons that motivate Christians to do good works. First, they help others because the love of God has captured their hearts. Christians feel compassion for those less fortunate than themselves, so they give their time, talent, and treasure to help the helpless. It's a supernatural internal motivation given by God that makes them reach out to others.

Second, gratitude is a driving motivation for Christians to help others. Count Nicholas von Zinzendorf, a young nobleman in Austria, was converted to Christ during the early 1700s. He saw a painting of the crucifixion of Jesus at the Dusseldorf Gallery with the motto: *Hoc feci pro te; Quid facis pro me?*, that is, "This I have done for you, what have you done for Me?" Zinzendorf determined to use all his resources to serve Christ. He opened his 12,000-acre estate to small bands of Christian refugees who were being persecuted all over Europe. Many at that time were persecuted, imprisoned, or had died for their faith. He named his community Herrnhutt—*The Lord's Watch*. Out of gratitude, Zinzendorf gave everything to help the persecuted. And out of gratitude, missionaries left Herrnhutt to go to Africa, India, and the colonies of America.

The third motivation is the command from the Bible, "Christians should be careful to do good deeds to all people, all the time" (Titus 3:8, author translation).

A fourth reason involves pragmatism. When Christians help others, they help themselves by the spiritual reason of growing in Christ and by the psychological reason that they feel good about themselves because they are truly *human*. (A person is not truly human until he recognizes the humanity of others.) But Christians also help themselves by contributing to a better society in which they live. If they help deliver a drug addict who steals to support his habit, the Christian is less likely to become a victim of a theft or mugging. Paul tells Titus, "Good work is good in itself and is also useful to mankind" (Titus 3:8, Phillips).

11

CHRISTIANITY IS A MOVEMENT THAT TRANSFORMS CULTURE

If a snowflake has feelings, it probably feels like it can't do much. One snowflake—different from all other flakes—has little influence on anything, but when millions of snowflakes get together, they can declare, "No school today!" Millions of snowflakes falling at the same time can announce, "No work today . . . no ball game . . ." Millions of snowflakes together can change the life of a city. What can Christians do when they get together?

Most Christians think they are powerless against the flood of evil found in the world. They reflect, "What can I do against the forces of abortion, hedonism, a sex-driven society, a pleasure-seeking population, and individuals who demand their civil rights to the exclusion of morality, truth, and group justice?"

Christians may feel alone, and they may even feel powerless, but together they can make a difference. The influence of Christians in the third century brought an end to the violent gladiator games and public execution of

Christians in the Colosseum. The growth of Christianity in the Roman Empire eventually led to the end of Caesar worship and the adoption of Christianity as an official religion in AD 313.

The greatest influence of Christianity is getting unbelieving people saved. But there is a second potential in Christianity that many Christians fail to recognize—the Christianization of culture. Throughout history, the widespread growth and influence of Christianity has transformed national and regional culture so that many cities have been known in history as Christian cities (e.g., London, England; Seoul, South Korea), regions have been known as Christian regions (e.g., Mizoram, India; Iona, Scotland), and nations have been known as Christian nations (e.g., Armenia; Great Britain; United States).

Today America is called a Christian nation, but any believer knows America is a long way from being Christian. But even with that understanding, there are still many evidences of Christian influence in America's laws, business practice, and the average way of American life. The Christian influences in American culture today are largely the remnants of an earlier time when biblical Christianity was a dominant influence on the formative culture of a young nation.

Throughout history, when revivals came to a region or country, their culture was influenced by Christian principles. When a nation is Christianized, it doesn't mean that everyone has become a Christian or that Christianity controls every citizen. It simply means the Christian principles and virtues have become a big influence upon that country's culture.

The Christianization of Ireland

In September 1857, James McQuilkin, a young Irishman, began a prayer meeting with three other men in the village schoolhouse near Kells. The four young men were concerned for the unbelievers in their community and began interceding for them by name at their weekly meeting. By December, the group rejoiced to see the first conversions among those on their prayer list. Many Irish church historians view that prayer meeting as the beginning of the Ulster revival.

Ulster is the northernmost province in Ireland. While McQuilkin and his friends gathered for prayer, other Christians throughout Ireland were doing the same. Throughout 1858, hundreds of prayer meetings were started, and many Irish preachers were speaking about revival in their sermons.

Early in 1859, the Spirit of God began to move in remarkable ways. In the midst of a crowded market in the town of Ballymena, a young man suddenly fell on his knees and cried out to God, "Unclean!" He began praying, "God be merciful to me, a sinner." This incident deeply influenced all who experienced it.

The incident in Ballymena quickly became known throughout the town. In response, Christians were invited to a special prayer meeting at the Ahoghill Presbyterian Church. The crowd that gathered on the evening of March 14 was larger than any had expected.

Those responsible for the maintenance of the building were concerned that the large crowd might put too much stress on the galleries. It became necessary that the building be cleared as a precaution. As a result, the crowd had to stand outside in a chilling rain as a layman preached with unusual spiritual power. By the end of the meeting, hundreds were kneeling on the wet ground in repentance, calling on God in prayer. The meeting was the first of many conducted throughout Ireland in the revival that followed.

According to some estimates, the revival that swept through Ireland in 1859 brought 100,000 converts into the churches. In both large and small meetings, people came under great conviction of sin. Often even physically strong people fell prostrate on the ground, unable to move for several hours. There was deep repentance and lasting change in lives that demonstrated the reality of the revival.

The phenomena that accompanied conviction in the Ulster revival were not nearly as dramatic as the social change growing out of the meetings. According to civic records, crime was greatly reduced in 1860, while judges in Ulster found themselves with no cases to try on several occasions. In County Antrim, it was reported that the police had no crimes to investigate and no prisoners in custody.

The Maze horse race typically drew 12,000 gamblers, but their numbers dwindled to 500. A Belfast whiskey distillery was listed for auction because of the decline in business. In Connor, the landlords of the local inns were converted, and they closed their pubs.

In short, according to some estimations, the Ulster revival "made a greater impact on Ireland than anything known since Patrick brought Christianity there." One observer described the effect of the revival in terms of "thronged services, unprecedented numbers of communicants, abundant prayer meetings, increased family prayers, unmatched Scripture reading, prosperous Sunday schools, converts remaining steadfast, increased giving, vice abated, and crime reduced."[15]

The Great Commission and the Transformation of Culture

Before returning to heaven, Jesus commanded His disciples, "Go into all the world and preach the Good News to everyone" (Mark 16:15, NLT). The disciples' primary focus was to preach the gospel to every person. But in Matthew's account of the Great Commission, given on a different occasion, the emphasis was different. "Go therefore and make disciples of all the nations, baptizing them in the name of the Father and of the Son and of the Holy Spirit" (Matt. 28:19). Here, the command to "make disciples of all the nations" (*mathïteusate panta ta ethnï*) points to the Christianization of a culture or society. While many readers think of "all the nations" in the context of individual political states within the global community, the Greek word *ethnï* is the root of our English word "ethnic." The nations mentioned in the Great Commission are better understood in the context of "ethnic groups" rather than political states. The word describes different people groups, such as the First Nations People of North America, the French Canadians of Quebec, and the American-born Chinese of San Francisco's Chinatown.

During the age of colonization, European missionaries assumed responsibility for both the evangelization and civilization of the people to whom they ministered. While their motives were right, their methods often left much to be desired. Rather than allowing the gospel to transform the culture it touched, they often imposed a European culture on a people struggling with the implications of the gospel in their own life. That strategy may have hindered the spread of the gospel as some who might have accepted the gospel did not because they did not want to adopt a European lifestyle in their tribal community.

To Christianize a nation is not to pass Christian laws, or force Christian baptism on everyone. Christianization does not start at the top and move down. Rather when Jesus Christ transforms individuals, they begin living for Christ in their homes and in their churches; then they begin to influence the larger society.

Some have described two contrasting methods of influencing society: the *trickle down* effect and the *bubble up* influence. The *trickle down* effect happens when a native chieftain of a tribe is converted and he decrees that everyone become a Christian. This also happens when a nation passes Christian-based laws that are imposed on everyone. Obviously, the *trickle down* effect is not the most effective.

The *bubble up* influence begins in the hearts of individuals when they are converted. Salvation transforms their values and attitudes. They desire righteousness, shun evil, and influence their families, their occupation, and those around them. The *bubble up* influence doesn't need laws passed to change people or society.

A nation is Christianized when society assumes Christian values and attitudes. A heathen jungle tribe stops murdering and men take only one wife instead of many. After a Christian revival, an area experiences less drunkenness and fewer family breakups. There is less crime when prostitutes are converted and thieves are born again.

There have been illustrations of the king of a tribe becoming a Christian. Then after the king was baptized, he commanded all his adherents to be baptized and become Christians (*trickle down* effect). While many tribe members may have had a heart transformation, others simply became Christians in name only. Because the king was now a Christian, certain Christian laws were passed. Over a period of time, the inward fleshly attitudes of professing Christians negatively influenced the Christian culture. That's only one reason why many nations that used to follow strong Christian principles are now Christian nations in "name only." Their culture has become more and more secular.

There are many illustrations of Roman Catholic kings sending out priests with explorers. The explorers were to conquer territories for the crown and get wealth for those who financed their expeditions, and the priests were to convert the heathen, thus making the area a Christian nation. To a large extent, the Spanish culture and Spanish religion, that is, the Roman Catholic Church, was forced on people of Latin America.

Making the Family Christian

Along with the Christianization of the *ethnes* (the nations), there is a second area of cultural influence by Christianity. It's the physical family group. The Greek word *oikos* is translated "family" or "household including servants and/or grandparents, grown unmarried children, or other relatives. Jesus cast the demons out of the man in Gadara, then told him, "Go home [*oikos*] to your friends, and tell them what great things the Lord has done for you" (Mark 5:19). This transformed man, previously controlled by demons, was sent to influence his family with the message of Jesus.

There are many illustrations of *oikos* conversions in the New Testament—Cornelius, the Philippian jailor, Lydia, Stephanus, etc. The mention of *oikos* conversions in the New Testament does not mean the father's conversion was applied to all members of his family. Nor is it a promise that the presence of one Christian in a family guarantees the eventual conversion of all other family members. Each person trusted Jesus for his or her personal salvation, and each person was converted separately. But usually when the father trusted Christ, everyone followed his example and came to a personal belief in Jesus Christ.

Today foreign missionaries call this a *people movement*, where many people make an individual decision to believe in Jesus Christ, but they make the same decision with others, simultaneously, and all become Christians. People movements are not found in our highly individualistic Western civilizations because people prize individuality and carefully weigh the influence of others before they follow the example of others. Hence, conversion is an individual experience in Western society. However, people movements still happen among primitive heathen tribes. They take place most often when the whole tribe has heard the gospel and has given it careful consideration. Then the decision of a leading member of that tribe to embrace Christianity opens the door for others to make the same decision.

The family unit is the most fundamental institution of society and the most effective way to pass on the core values of one generation to the next. When the gospel effects the conversion of families, it often changes the core values of that family. Paul reminded the Corinthians, "If anyone is in Christ, he is a new creation; old things have passed away; behold, all things have become new" (2 Cor. 5:17). This transformation of culture through the family is seen in two particular phenomena, which accompany conversion.

Historians use the expression "the Protestant work ethic" to describe the impact of the Protestant Reformation and rise of the middle class in Europe following that religious movement. Family values changed in many homes touched by Protestantism, and a major change was the attitude toward work and leisure. Protestant ministers taught people that their primary goal in life was to glorify God. They understood, "Whether you eat or drink, or whatever you do, do all to the glory of God" (1 Cor. 10:31). As a result, when Christians gathered together for worship, the passive approach to worship they had known in the celebration of the Mass was replaced with a more active involvement as they sought to glorify God through congregational singing and the preaching of the Scriptures. The rest of the week, they expended an equal amount of energy glorifying God by working hard. The immediate impact of the Protestant work ethic was a higher level of productivity.

Sociologists today describe "redemption and lift" as a secondary impact of that work ethic. In a free enterprise society, those who work the hardest are rewarded financially. Because Christians will probably work hard, they might prosper more than others. One additional effect of their conversion was moral improvement. Money that Christians previously spent on vices was now available to spend on and with the family. Often, this took the form of buying a home in a nicer neighborhood, purchasing a more reliable vehicle to drive, providing healthier, nutritional food for their family, and financing better education and health care for their children. To put it in the vernacular, "When people get saved, they get better."

What happens in a family impacts the community at large. When many families in a city pass through this process of Christianization, the quality of life in that city is raised. In the first century, when the gospel was preached and embraced in a Samaritan city, "there was great joy in that city" (Acts 8:8). When the same process is widely experienced in a nation, that nation experiences the blessing of God. "Blessed is the nation whose God is the LORD, the people He has chosen as His own inheritance" (Ps. 33:12).

Saving the World from Itself

Whenever Christianity touches a culture in a significant way, there is always a change in a positive way. Real Christians advocate social justice for their current society. The abolition of slavery, prison reform, the care of widows and orphans, and the development of hospitals and schools are some of the historic reforms that find their roots in the historic faith of biblical Christianity.

That does not mean the mere presence of Christians in a community will transform the culture. Cultural transformation only takes place when Christians consistently live out their faith and allow their values to be governed by biblical principles. When that doesn't happen, Jesus describes those followers as salt that has lost its flavor and are "good for nothing but to be trampled underfoot by men" (Matt. 5:13). Karl Marx called Christianity "the opiate of the people" because he failed to see Christians allowing their faith to motivate them to address the social problems in London, England. Mahatma Gandhi studied Christianity and the teachings of Jesus in South Africa at a time when Christians refused to address the issue of apartheid and concluded, "I would be a Christian if it were not for Christians."

How different from the transformational movement described in the New Testament. There the enemies of Christianity were forced to admit, "These who have turned the world upside down have come here too" (Acts 17:6). The source of Christianity's power to change cultures is found in another description of those early Christians: "They realized that they had been with Jesus" (Acts 4:13). That kind of Christianity has always resulted in positive social change. As a result, Christianity has most often been a transformational movement. It's only when the influence of an evangelical revival begins addressing moral problems and applying biblical principles, will there be lasting solutions.

It does not take many to begin the transformation of a culture, but it does take intense dedication. When revival came to an Anglican church in Clapham, London, England, one man touched by that revival, William Wilberforce, became concerned over the widespread practice of slavery. He devoted the rest of his life to working for the abolition of slavery in England and her colonies. Through years of hard work, he was able to organize others who shared his belief that slavery was wrong. Just days before his death, buying, selling, or owning slaves became illegal in the British Empire.

More recently, significant social reforms have been affected by Christian leaders. The name of Dr. Martin Luther King Jr. is synonymous with the success of America's civil rights movement. Bishop Desmond Tutu provided moral leadership in South Africa, bringing that country's apartheid doctrine to an end. Christians around the world today are engaged in efforts to protect human life by seeking to change laws that legalize abortion and euthanasia, to bring an end to pornography and the child sex trade in some countries, and to oppose state-sponsored gambling that leaves so many homeless and without resources to meet their most basic needs.

The Old Testament book of Judges describes a series of cultural reforms followed by moral decline in Israel. That pattern is typical of the reforming influence of Christianity and illustrates the relationship between revival and reform. During historical periods of revival, Christians have established schools, hospitals, and housing for the poor, advocated prison reform and temperance, and established societies or organizations to carry out these objectives. But a generation later, these causes are not widely supported. The writer of Judges describes this reality with the words "another generation arose after them who did not know the LORD nor the work which He had done for Israel" (Judg. 2:10). The work of God that motivates one generation to greatness is lost on the next generation that has not experienced it.

The mandate of the Great Commission calls for the making of disciples. When large numbers of people are converted to Christ during times of revival, the renewed commitment to God means Christians are more likely than usual to assume a responsibility in discipling new believers. As the gospel begins changing individual lives, those individuals begin changing the culture in which they live. What happened in the Ulster Revival and Protestant Reformation is typical of great revival movements throughout history.

But what about life after the revival subsides? Sadly, without the atmosphere of revival, many Christians lapse into something inferior to the Christian norm. Christian culture declines. But even in the darker hours of a declining culture, God has always had His people. Even today, in an age when it seems Christianity has so little direct influence on contemporary Western culture, deeply committed Christians and Christian organizations are in the forefront of humanitarian programs to feed the poor (famine relief worldwide and breakfast programs in America), treat the sick (AIDS education in Africa and drug rehabilitation programs in America), and promote social reform (prison reform and literacy projects). Could these be the seeds that will flourish in the next outpouring of the Holy Spirit and give rise to the next cultural transformation in history?

12

CHRISTIANITY IS A GLOBAL DIRECTIVE

Five young missionary families in their twenties went to evangelize the Waorani Indians (referred to at the time as the Auca Indians) in Ecuador during the fall of 1956. Why would these college-educated young people bury their lives in the jungles of South America when they had so much going for them? The Ecuadorian government had determined to eliminate the tribe because of their fierceness to the other tribes about them, so the young men had to work fast.

They had a yellow Piper Cruiser plane and planned to land on the sand bar in the middle of the Curaray River in the dry season before the winter floods covered their landing strip. The five young men had been leaving gifts to make friends with the tribes. The Indians didn't understand their friendship, and hacked all five men to death.

It's often said that the blood of martyrs becomes the seed for the church. God honored the faith of these five men and eventually the gospel reached the tribe and most of them became Christians. In August 2000, I heard Mincaye[16] speak at the Billy Graham conference on evangelism in Amsterdam. He admitted being one of those who clubbed the missionaries to death. Mincaye told of now being an elder in a church that had evangelized its community.

Rachel Saint, wife to the martyred Nate Saint, went back to that tribe, accompanied by her children to be raised in that tribe, and helped spread the gospel among the natives. She didn't run back to the United States in bitterness, but determined that her husband didn't die in vain. Her son, who was raised among the Aucas, became the human instrument that transformed the Auca Indians.

The Auca Indians' language was reduced to writing, and the New Testament was translated into their language. The men who clubbed the missionaries to death were taught to read so they could understand God's Word. Today there is a thriving church among the Auca Indians. The tribe has been civilized, and once again, light has triumphed over darkness.

Why would five young men bury their lives in a heathen jungle? Because Christ commanded His followers to preach the gospel message to every person (Mark 16:15). Why would Steve Saint, Rachel's son, spend his life transforming one pagan culture into one with Christian values?[17] Because Jesus commanded, "Teaching them to observe all things that I have commanded you" (Matt. 28:20). The original disciples obeyed Jesus' Great Commission. They went everywhere preaching the gospel, and they died for their faith.

As the first century of the early church era came to a close, most of the twelve apostles who followed Jesus had fulfilled the commission He gave them and died violent deaths. The church that they had humanly established was spread throughout the known world. According to an early church tradition, the twelve apostles divided up the known world and as witnesses took the gospel "to the end of the earth" (Acts 1:8).

Scholars generally believe Andrew ministered in Asia Minor, traveling as far north as Scythia near the Black Sea in what is now southern Russia, and that he was eventually crucified in Achaia. Because Andrew felt unworthy to die on the same kind of cross on which Jesus died, he was apparently bound to an X-shaped cross that has been preserved in the national flag of Scotland as St. Andrew's Cross.

Philip is also said to have ministered in Asia Minor, but apparently the major focus of his ministry was in Galatia and perhaps among the Gauls in France. Philip is the only one of the twelve apostles associated with France in any way. Philip apparently was stoned, then crucified at Hieropolis.

It appears Bartholomew took the gospel to Armenia and gave birth to the church in that nation. Armenia was the first Christian nation in history and a strong Armenian Christian church still exists. Bartholomew was beaten and crucified in Albania.

Thomas seems to have preached as far east as India. There is a strong Indian tradition that the Mar Thomas Church in India was founded by that apostle in AD 52 when he landed at Cranganore and was instrumental in the conversion of several high-caste Hindu families in the area. His life and ministry apparently ended in martyrdom in or near Mylapore on the coast of India.

Matthew apparently ministered in Ethiopia and in Persia. He probably died in Egypt, having been condemned and martyred by the Sanhedrin. Scholars do not agree on the reference to the death of Matthew in the Talmud.

James, the son of Alphaeus, ministered in Syria but was eventually martyred in Jerusalem.

Simon the Zealot preached across North Africa and up the Atlantic coast of Europe as far as Britain. He then traveled to Syria and preached the gospel there until he was captured and sawed in half.

Judas Thaddaeus, it seems, preached the gospel in Edessa and Armenia and was killed with arrows at the foot of Mount Ararat.

The twelve apostles obeyed the commands of Jesus, just as the five martyrs in Ecuador did, and just as millions of other followers of Jesus have. And still today, missionaries are passionate to preach the gospel in every ethnic group and heathen tribe. They feel their job will not be completed until everyone has heard the gospel.

The command was to capture the hearts of all people, not to militarily capture nations as did the Crusaders and the explorers from Christian nations in the sixteenth and seventeenth centuries. The command was not to enforce Christian laws on a group of unwilling subjects, but to love each person as God loved them, so that all willingly submitted to God's love.

The Command of Jesus to Go

Jesus did not give Himself to mass evangelism; rather He devoted Himself primarily to training His disciples and equipping them to do the work of evangelism. It all began with approximately "five hundred brethren" (1 Cor. 15:6) who saw Jesus after His resurrection.

When Jesus first appeared to His ten disciples in the Upper Room on Easter Sunday afternoon, He gave them the embryonic elements of the Great Commission, "As the Father has sent Me, I also send you" (John 20:21). The disciples might have asked, "To whom shall we go?" Jesus hadn't yet told them to go into all the world. They also could have asked, "What shall we preach?" Jesus hadn't yet told them to preach the gospel of His death and resurrection. They could have asked as well, "What shall we accomplish?" Jesus hadn't yet told them about gathering believers into the church—the body of Christ.

Jesus met His disciples a week later while there were eleven in the Upper Room (Mark 16:14). Jesus began to answer their questions when he said, "Go into all the world and preach the gospel to every creature" (Mark 16:15). They were not to just go to the Jews, but to everyone. They were not to just preach the kingdom of heaven they heard in Jesus' earthly life, but they were to preach the gospel, the good news that Jesus died for their sins, and He arose again to give new life.

Two or three weeks later, Jesus met His disciples again near a mountain in Galilee (Matt. 28:16). Then He gave them a complete statement of the Great Commission: "Go therefore and make disciples of all the nations, baptizing them in the name of the Father and of the Son and of the Holy Spirit, teaching them to observe all things that I have commanded you; and lo, I am with you always, even to the end of the age. Amen" (Matt. 28:19–20).

The word *go* could be translated, "as you are going." Jesus assumed they would be going. The command was to "make disciples." The word *disciple* means "to be a follower." Just as the disciples had followed Jesus, they would now make followers out of every nation.

Each one who followed Jesus Christ was to be baptized by a Trinitarian formula— "in the name of the Father, Son, and Holy Spirit." In the final aspect of the commission, they were to teach each new follower of Christ everything that Jesus had taught them.

Some ask, "To whom is the Great Commission given?" Obviously in the context, Jesus meant the eleven disciples. But at the end of the commission Jesus said, "I am with you always, even to the end of the age," which clearly meant all of His other true followers throughout time. This means Jesus gave the Great Commission to the total body of believers to evangelize the lost (unbelievers).

Paul understood the Great Commission involved every believer when he said, "Therefore, we are ambassadors for Christ, as though God were making an appeal through us; we beg you on behalf of Christ, be reconciled to God" (2 Cor. 5:20). Notice the word *beg*. Paul was imploring believers to witness with passion and expect results. This was evident in Paul's presentation to King Agrippa, who hearing the emotional appeal of Paul said, "Almost thou persuadest me to be a Christian" (Acts 26:28, KJV).

Apparently, the early church understood the mandate. It is said of them, "And daily in the temple, and in every house, they did not cease teaching and preaching Jesus as the Christ" (Acts 5:42).

And notice the places where the Jerusalem church evangelized. They did it in homes, marketplaces, synagogues, jails, before rulers and kings, and everywhere throughout the city. They took the gospel everywhere so much that the high priest said, "Ye have filled Jerusalem with your doctrine" (Acts 5:28). And what was the result of their aggressive, bold evangelism? "And believers were the more added to the Lord, multitudes both of men and women" (Acts 5:14).

Every Christian should ask the questions, "Why am I here?" "Why didn't God take me home when I got saved?" The answer to that is God wants you to reach other people for Christ, and bring them with you when you go to your home in heaven.

Not only must individual Christians win others to Christ, it is also the task of local churches. The Great Commission involves baptizing people "in the name of the Father, Son and Holy Spirit"; this is a church ordinance. All believers are placed in the universal body of Christ at salvation, and they should identify with a local church (the local body of Christ). The church is God's instrument to mobilize His people for evangelism, to encourage them to do it, and motivate them to the noble task of sharing the gospel with everyone in the world.

The local church carries out its evangelistic obligation by praying for lost people to come to Christ, by giving money to support missionaries, by being involved in projects to evangelize, and by sending its young people as missionaries. Local churches do these activities out of love for Jesus Christ and a compassion for people. While some treat it as an obligaion or burden, a passion for world evangelism is one of the defining characteristics of a biblical church.

There are two imperatives in the Great Commission. The first is *evangelism* and the second is *education*. These two activities have always had tension. The imperative "go" means that the primary thrust of evangelism must be done outside the church building. Many people in the church feel that the pastor does evangelism in his sermons. But the

Great Commission is intended for all members as they go outside the church building into the marketplace.

Numerous churches have given themselves to a strong teaching ministry, in small group ministries as well as their pulpit ministry, yet the primary imperative of the Great Commission is to "make disciples." This means helping men and women to become devoted followers of Jesus Christ and serving Him through the church.

A contemporary problem is that Christianity now focuses on "building-centered evangelism." Americans spend evangelistic energy on "inviting evangelism." This means that the only people who will be won to Christ are those who deliberately attend church and willingly expose themselves to the message of the gospel. But what about the vast majority of people who will not go into a church building and will not be exposed to the gospel?

The present-day church must follow the New Testament principle of being both a *gathering* body and a *scattering* body. The church must *gather* for teaching, fellowship, and worship, but it also must *scatter* to spread the Word of God to their relatives, their neighborhoods, and the marketplace. Notice what the early church did: "Therefore those who were scattered went everywhere preaching the word" (Acts 8:4).

Jesus gave two parables about the kingdom of heaven that apply to current church strategy. Jesus likens evangelism to inviting guests to attend a wedding (Matt. 22:1–14). In verse 9, there is the command to go, find people, and invite them to the wedding feast. The second parable involves a certain man who gives a dinner party and invites many to come (Luke 14:16–24). But when the guests will not come, the host gives a command to his servants to go out and bring them in (Luke 14:21). When he didn't have enough people, he again commanded, "Go out into the highways and along the hedges, and compel them to come in, so that my house may be filled" (Luke 14:23). This means the church must reach outside its doors into the community to invite people to salvation.

The Message

When Jesus began His ministry, His invitation was very simple, "Follow Me, and I will make you become fishers of men" (Mark 1:17). So, the disciples became followers of Jesus Christ with the purpose of catching others so they too would follow Jesus.

After the death and resurrection of Jesus Christ, these events became the core message of the gospel—the good news that Jesus died for all and arose to give life. The word *gospel* is found seventy-six times in the New Testament. Originally, the term *gospel* in the Anglo-Saxon culture was *God spell*, meaning *God-story*. The gospel is the great story of God coming to redeem the human race.

The verb *evangelize* means to announce or proclaim good news. It appears fifty-one times in the New Testament and is the verb form of the noun *gospel*. When a person evangelizes another person, he is pouring the gospel into him or her.

Another word is *witness*. Right before returning to heaven Jesus said, "And you shall be witnesses to Me in Jerusalem, and in all Judea and Samaria, and to the end of the earth" (Acts 1:8). *Witness* is primarily a legal term among the New Testament Greeks that meant telling the truth about facts and events they had observed. Witnessing involved personal involvement of telling others what they had experienced. That means when someone witnesses about Jesus Christ, he shares how he became a Christian, and what Christ means to him now.

As one traces the word *witness* through the book of Acts, it meant more than simply presenting what a person has observed. It means personal attesting to the message of Jesus' death and resurrection by giving evidence that one's life has been changed by the gospel. For that reason, witnessing describes a combination of the facts of the gospel with one's personal experience. As Jesus explained the message of the gospel, "You are witnesses of these things" (Luke 24:48).

A Christian witnesses to others by the way he lives. If he expresses the fruit of the Spirit, he will be loving, joyful, peaceable, patient, gentle, good, faithful, meek, and self-disciplined (Gal. 5:22–23). When he is controlled by the Holy Spirit, it won't be long before others will realize there is something special about him, and that he is the kind of person they enjoy knowing. The ultimate goal of silent witnessing is to get others to want the type of life that is lived by the Christian.

A believer also witnesses by the way he talks. Profanity, gossip, foolish jesting, telling dirty jokes, constant complaining, and other sins of the mouth drive people away from Christ. That's the negative part, however; there is also a positive aspect. A believer is expected to talk about good things, especially the things of the Lord and His Word. New converts often find it difficult to keep quiet about their salvation experience. In contrast, those who have been saved a long time often find it difficult to say anything about their experience. Witnessing should be a lifelong habit for all Christians.

Witnessing begins by giving a testimony—telling what God has done for and to you as a person. You share about your life before you became a believer, telling how you came to Christ, and what Christ means to you now. Your testimony may be a natural entrance to presenting the gospel, and your witness may open the door to soul winning.

Remember, all evangelism eventually comes down to a one-to-one encounter between a person seeking Christ and a Christian showing him the way. Every believer should know how to lead a person to Christ.

Evangelism also carries the idea of taking the initiative and seeking those who need to be saved. Jesus said, "I am the good shepherd. The good shepherd gives His life for the sheep" (John 10:11). Like the shepherd, the Christian must give his life to seek lost sheep to tell them of the gospel. Jesus gave the parable of the man who has a hundred sheep, but one is lost. What does he do? He leaves "the ninety-nine . . . and goes after the one which is lost until he finds it" (Luke 15:4). What did this mean to Jesus? "I say to you that likewise there will be more joy in heaven over one sinner who repents than over ninety-nine just persons who need no repentance" (Luke 15:7). And what does the shepherd do when he finds that one? "And when he comes home, he calls together his friends and neighbors, saying to them, 'Rejoice with me, for I have found my sheep which was lost!' " (Luke 15:6). This is an illustration of how God expects His children to evangelize.

So, evangelism is an intentional effort to reach unbelievers. If an individual drops his keys while opening a door, simply looking for the keys is not enough. He must continue looking for them until he finds them, or he'll remain locked out. Some "lost sheep" don't want to be found, so a Christian must do all he can do to find them and win them to Christ. And what does this involve? This involves doing good works to soften their hearts. This involves living a godly life before them so that they will see in a person's life both the Savior and fruits of righteousness. This involves praying for them so God will draw them to salvation.

All evangelistic intention should be done with urgency. Why? People are lost and there is real punishment in a real hell awaiting them. Also, they must know God loves them and has a wonderful plan for their life.

Think about It

Question: Christianity spreads as believers give the gospel to non-Christians. What is the primary motive of Christians to evangelize non-Christians?

Answer: Each Christian is motivated by a different response to God; each response may be triggered by different needs in the life of the believer. First, a Christian should tell others that God loves them because God's love is so great. "The love of Christ forces us to tell others the gospel" (2 Cor. 5:14, author translation). A second reason is to be obedient to the commands of Christ (Acts 7:8). A third reason is because of one's love for the person to whom we are witnessing. A fourth reason is the rewards a Christian will receive when he meets Christ in heaven (1 Thess. 2:19–20).

But there is also a negative reason—Christians will lose their rewards at the judgment seat of Christ if they do not faithfully witness for Him on this earth (2 Cor. 5:10–11).

Whatever the reason, Christians must let their light shine to influence others (Matt. 5:14–16). One dominant characteristic of Christianity is that it involves evangelism throughout the world.

13

CHRISTIANITY IS AN ULTIMATE HOPE

Deep in the heart of every person is a desire for life beyond death and a belief that there is a paradise after the grave. Even those people who deny hell talk about heaven. About one hundred years ago there was a song that proclaimed, "*Everybody Talkin' 'Bout Heaven (that ain't goin' there).*"[18]

Abraham, the man identified as living by faith, "Looked for a city . . . whose builder and maker is God" (Heb. 11:10, KJV). Abraham did not possess that city on this earth, but "died in faith." But throughout his life he "looked for a city" just as a family moving into a new neighborhood will look forward to the details of their new home and neighborhood in which they will live. So, most Christians not only expect a life after death, but they want to know about the place they will spend all eternity.

The night before Jesus died, He told His disciples that He was going away; but they didn't understand where He was going. He then told them plainly He was going to heaven. "In My Father's house are many mansions . . . I go to prepare a place for you" (John 14:2). While this mansion in heaven may be a perfect place to live, there are only brief descriptions of it in the Bible. The most important distinction is not the furniture or the construction of the home in heaven, but the fact that believers will live with God. Jesus said, "I will come again and receive you to Myself; that where I am, there you may be also" (John 14:3).

Paul describes the coming of Jesus Christ and heaven as "a blessed hope." This is a hope that applies to all Christians. Christ will return to take them to heaven to live with Him. Paul exhorted believers to be "looking for the blessed hope and glorious appearing of our great God and Savior Jesus Christ" (Titus 2:13).

Peter said we were born again "to a living hope . . . to an inheritance incorruptible and undefiled . . . reserved in heaven for you" (1 Pet. 1:3–4). Peter wrote a letter calling it a "living hope," because this assurance lives within the heart of all believers. Every believer should live with confidence that when he dies, he will go to live with God.

There are some who define heaven in terms of a good life on this earth. They feel that all the good things that happen to Christians today are heaven. They interpret the Bible mystically that the "new heaven" and "new earth" is a better life after one is converted. However, a clear interpretation of Scripture teaches that a believer's hope is not on this earth, but it is a life with God in heaven after death.

Location of Heaven

No one is certain as to the exact location of heaven. However, as we examine all the references to heaven, we find there is more than one heaven. "Jesus passed through the heavens" (Heb. 4:14), and "He ascended far above all the heavens" (Eph. 4:10). Paul thought there were at least three heavens; he testified of "being caught up to the third heaven" (2 Cor. 12:1–4).

The first heaven is the atmosphere about us, that is, the air that surrounds humans and all created life on this earth (Matt. 6:26; James 5:18). The second heaven is the stellar outer space where planets and stars are located (Matt. 24:29; Gen. 15:5). The third heaven is described as the dwelling place of God (2 Cor. 12:2). While there is such a place, there is much that is unknown about this heaven, except it is a place where God is located (Rev. 3:12; 20:9).

While it's popular for some to say that this heaven is nothing more than a state of bliss, that view cannot be harmonized with biblical teaching. The Bible explicitly states there is a real place called heaven, where real people will spend a real eternity.

The physical presence of Jesus Christ is one of the best arguments that heaven is a real place. When Christ arose from the dead, He did so in the same human body that hung on the cross; however, it was a resurrected body with new life. Since deity and humanity are indissolubly united into one single person, an individual cannot say that Christ's soul went to heaven and not His body. Throughout all eternity Christ will have a body: "This man . . . continues forever" (Heb. 7:24). Therefore, there must be a real heaven where a real physical Christ dwells throughout all eternity.

While Paul talks about three heavens, there technically is a fourth heaven mentioned in Scripture. It comes into existence in the future when "the first heaven and the first earth had passed away" (Rev. 21:1).

The key to understanding this new heaven is the word *new*. The fourth heaven will be more than new in time or sequence; it will be new in substance. The present material earth and heaven will not be annihilated, but transformed. The Bible speaks about "the heavens will pass away . . . both the earth and the works that are in it will be burned up" (2 Pet. 3:10). This means this present earth will be burned up and be transformed into something wholly new.

Our Hope

No one wants to die; usually we pass from this life into the next with pain and suffering. Who likes to suffer? Yet, everyone hopes for some kind of life on the other side. While that may be a pipe dream for most, the Christian has an empirical basis for "hoping" for a life after death. The Christian's hope does not arise from his desire or wishes; rather it comes from God Himself, who gives the believer the gift of hope.

This hope is more than one's hope in God, as the psalmist said, "My hope is in You" (Ps. 39:7). God implants hope into the Christians' heart so they exercise the anticipation given them by God. Peter describes, "The hope that is in you" (1 Pet. 3:15). John describes it, "Everyone who has this hope in him" (1 John 3:3). This Christian hope of the future comes from God: "Now may the God of hope fill you with all joy and peace in believing, that you may abound in hope by the power of the Holy Spirit" (Rom. 15:13). So hope not only comes from God, but when Christians receive it, they reverse their hope back toward

God who gave it to them in the first place. Paul said, "I have hope in God" (Acts 24:15).

The Christian with hope is distinguished from the unbeliever who has no hope (Eph 2:12; 1 Thess. 4:13). This hope is only available to the believers, for it is a reciprocal relationship between the Christian and Christ.

Christians' hope is not wishful thinking they will go to heaven, but a firm assurance that God has promised to be with them in this life, and to give them eternal life in heaven when they die.

And what is the fruit of the Christians' hope? Our hope is confident because we have eternal life (Titus 1:2; 3:7); our salvation is secure (1 Thess. 5:8); we will meet Christ at His appearing (Titus 2:13); our bodies will be resurrected (Acts 23:6; 26:6–7); and our bodies will be transformed and glorified to live with God forever (Phil. 3:21; 1 Cor. 15:51–59).

Hope produces steadfastness in the present life (Rom. 5:4). Therefore, it is called an "anchor of hope" that keeps one from discouragement and disappointment (Heb. 6:18–20). If a Christian didn't have this hope in the middle of troubles and sufferings, he or she might give up physically, or worse, even deny one's faith. But the prospect of a glorious future life keeps a Christian going in the midst of today's present tribulations.

When a Christian gets to heaven, he will still exercise his hope, for he will continually look forward to better things. Notice the passage in 1 Corinthians 13:13, "And now abide faith, hope, love, these three." Paul said earlier, "Whether there are prophecies, they will fail; whether there are tongues, they will cease; whether there is knowledge, it will vanish away" (1 Cor. 13:8). So certain things will eventually pass away, but not faith, hope, and love. The word "abide" is in contrast to the things that "will vanish away," suggesting that these three—faith, hope, and love—are eternal attitudes that will endure in the next world.

The permanence of faith, hope, and love in the next world is not easily understood. As a matter of fact, very little is known about what believers will do on the other side of death. But faith, hope, and love are so essential to Christian character, that it is unthinkable for the Christian to live in the next life without them. This means that the Christian's life in heaven will not be static, but he or she will have opportunities for unlimited growth. A Christian's faith can grow throughout eternity to trust God even more. Thus, the believer can have a stronger hope and can grow even deeper in love with God.

The trees on either side of the river that flows from the throne of God will bear fruit twelve months each year, and "the leaves of the tree are for the growth of the nations" (Rev. 22:2, author translation). In heaven, Christians will grow in their personal character and in their response to God. They will grow in their faith, hope, and love. In their growth they will be sinless and in a sense be *perfect* but they will never be perfect like God, for only God is perfect.

A Description of Heaven

Heaven will be a perfect place, but a person will never completely appreciate this perfection on earth because one's understanding is so limited. Why is that? First, the glory of that eternal home is described in human language— words cannot adequately describe heaven. When Paul was caught up into the third heaven he explained, "That he was caught up into Paradise, and heard inexpressible words, which it is not lawful for a man to utter" (2 Cor. 12:4). Apparently, Paul could not completely express what he saw in heaven, and God didn't want him to tell anyone; so, God gave Paul a physical problem so that he would be constantly reminded that he shouldn't tell any man what he saw. "Lest I should be exalted above measure by the abundance of the revelations, a thorn in the flesh was given to me . . . to buffet me, lest I be exalted above measure" (2 Cor. 12:7).

The Bible describes heaven in terms of earthly treasures and beauties—pearls, diamonds, rubies, etc. The splendor and beauty of heaven far outshine anything the human mind can comprehend. An individual will not be able to understand it until he arrives there. But beyond tangible things such as gold and silver, notice the inexhaustible blessings of heaven:

- abundant life (1 Tim. 4:8)
- rest (Rev. 14:13)
- knowledge (1 Cor. 13:8–10)
- holiness (Rev. 21:27)
- serving God (Rev. 22:3)
- worship (Rev. 19:1)
- fellowship with God (Rev. 21:3)
- fellowship with other believers (1 Thess. 4:8)
- glory (2 Cor. 4:17).

The greatest quality of heaven is the fact of the presence of God. John said, "I saw no temple in it, for the Lord God Almighty and the Lamb are its temple" (Rev. 21:22).

The word *temple* is symbolic of the presence of God. John described it as, "The tabernacle of God is with men, and He will dwell with them" (Rev. 21:3). Just as in the Old Testament, the Shekinah glory cloud entered the tabernacle to indicate the symbolic presence of God was there; heaven is described as a place "having the glory of God" (Rev. 21:11).

Heaven is eternal and will be inhabited by those who have eternal life (Titus 1:2; 3:7). The believer is promised an eternal inheritance (Heb. 9:15), therefore there must be an eternal place where the Christian can enjoy this inheritance.

Heaven is described as having no day or night because day and night are sequences that measure time. So in heaven there is "no need of the sun or of the moon" (Rev. 21:23).

There will be no death in heaven. Remember, death means separation of the body and soul, so no believer will die in heaven because he will be forever joined to God. John has said, "Then Death . . . w[as] cast into the lake of fire" (Rev. 20:14).

Heaven has no disappointments, failures, or regrets. "And God will wipe away every tear from their eyes; there shall be no more death, nor sorrow, nor crying. There shall be no more pain, for the former things have passed away" (Rev. 21:4).

Over the years, our interest and attitude toward heaven change. When we were young, we thought of living for God, but our life was centered on the challenges of every day. The older we become, the closer we get to moving into heaven. Therefore, those of us who are older are most concerned about knowing every detail about the biblical doctrine of heaven. Yes, every Christian knows he will go to heaven when he dies. But the closer we get to it, the more real it becomes to us. But in the final analysis, the destination of heaven is not as important as the fact that we will live with God for eternity. And that is the ultimate hope of every Christian.

Think about It

Question: Why would God give His children assurance that they will go to live with Him after they die?

Answer: If God's children know where they will spend eternity, then they tend to work harder for Him on this earth. Also, they are more willing to sacrifice to please Him on this earth. And, when they know their future is secure, they will better worship and praise Him on this earth. After all, this life is preparatory for the next life, so the good things God gives us down here are only a taste of the good things that await us in heaven.

ENDNOTES

❖

1. Flavius Josephus, *The Works of Flavius Josephus,* translated by William Whiston (Boston: Dewolfe, Fiske and Company, 1883), p. 474.

2. http://www.why-the-bible.com/intellect.htm (accessed 4 April 2005).

3. Elmer L. Towns, *The Names of Jesus* (Denver: Accent Publications, 1989).

4. A. M. Hodgkin, *Christ in All the Scriptures,* 6th ed. (London: Pickering, 1922).

5. See http://www.wycliffe.org/.

6. http://www.errantskeptics.org/Quotes_by_Presidents .htm#John%20Adams (accessed 21 April 2005).

7. John Dick, *Lectures on Theology* (New York: Robert Carter and Brothers, 1878), 2:106.

8. Richard Riss, *The Evidence for the Resurrection of Jesus Christ* (Minneapolis: Bethany Fellowship, 1977), 62.

9. http://dictionary.reference.com/search?q=conversion, s.v. "conversion" (accessed 17 October 2005).

10. Elmer L. Towns, *How to Pray: When You Don't Know What to Say* (Ventura, CA: Regal Books), 2006.

11. Elmer L. Towns, *Praying the Lord's Prayer for Spiritual Breakthrough* (Ventura, CA: Regal Books), 1997.

12. "In the heavenlies" is the key phrase of the book of Ephesians. This book begins by describing all the benefits a believer has "in Christ" in heaven. The believer should "walk

worthily" on earth because of the things God has for him in heaven.

13. http://www.m-w.com/dictionary/epoch, s.v. "epoch" (accessed 1 November 2005).

14. Westminster Shorter Catechism, http://www.reformed.org/documents/larger1.html (accessed 31 October 2005).

15. This report taken from *The Ten Greatest Revivals Ever* (Ann Arbor, MI: Servant Publications, 2000), 125–126.

16. See Arches Unbound, "Mysterious Ways," http://www2 .ups.edu/arches/2004Fall/featureMysteriousWays.html (accessed 14 November 2005). This story was reported by Mary Boone.

17. Elisabeth Elliot, *Through Gates of Splendor*, (Carol Stream, IL: Tyndale House, 1995). This tells the story of five missionaries who sacrificed their lives in the jungles of Ecuador. A documentary film released in 2004, *Beyond the Gates of Splendor*, available on DVD, takes us through that original journey to the events that followed half a century after, http://www.beyondthegatesthemovie.com, (accessed 27 November 2005).

18. Words and music: George Pendergrass and John Green © 1993 Anthony K. Music (ASCAP) / Clifty Music (BMI).

BIBLIOGRAPHY

Heitzig, Skip. *Jesus Up Close*. Wheaton, IL: Tyndale House Publishers Inc., 2001.

Little, Paul E. *Know Why You Believe*. Wheaton, IL: Victor Books, 1976.

McDowell, Josh. *Evidence That Demands A Verdict*. San Bernardino, CA: Campus Crusade for Christ International, 1972.

Riss, Richard. *The Evidence for the Resurrection of Jesus Christ*. Minneapolis: Bethany Fellowship Inc., 1977.

Strobel, Lee. *The Case for Christ*. Grand Rapids, MI: Zondervan Publishing House, 1998.

Towns, Elmer L. *Concise Bible Doctrines*. Chattanooga, TN: AMG Publishers, 2006.

Yancey, Philip. *The Jesus I Never Knew*. Grand Rapids, MI: Zondervan Publishing House, 1995.